What Others Are Saying

The Red Book is a breath of fresh air, a commanding call to action, and an invitation for the church to take children's ministry seriously so we can make a difference like never before! This book is a must-read for anyone who ministers to children and families in the church.

Ryan Frank
Author of *The Volunteer Code*
and CEO/Publisher at Kidzmatter

For thirty years and counting Mark Harper has been my friend. He's not just a person I know, he's someone I trust. He's not just been a children's pastor he's the kind of children's pastor that has produced spiritual champions. Mark is a walking google of children's ministry. Not only does he know a bunch of info about children's ministry he knows what matters most and that's what this book is all about. Whether you are new to children's ministry or are a veteran yourself this book will sharpen you and help you understand not just what's good or helpful but what's essential. This book needed to be written years ago but it took Mark years to learn it. Now you can learn it without taking years or learning it the hard way. I've said this for years, "Experience is the best teacher but it doesn't have to be your experiences that your learn from." *The Red Book* is packed full of practical, hands-on experience from one of the best I know.

Jim Wideman
Children's & Family Ministry Pioneer,
Author, Coach, Orange Thinker

Mark Harper has been a voice of influence in children's ministry for decades. In his new book, *The Red Book,* he shares his years of wisdom in an easy to read and apply format. *The Red Book* isn't about everything in kid's ministry, it's about the things that matter most. Every chapter is chocked full of principles that will help you make sure your kid's ministry is focused on the right thing and on the right person, Jesus.

Jason Martin
Executive Family Pastor
at Element Church in Wentzville, MO

The Red Book is a must read for any children's ministry leader. A great foundation for those just staring out and vital insights for those who are seasoned veterans. Mark's experience and passion for ministry shines bright in this vital resource for leaders.

John & Crystal McLennan
Children's Pastors at CT Church in Houston, Texas

Everyone needs help now and then, but not everyone has some to turn to in those times. *The Red Book* can help in those moments! A lot of resources deal with what is going on now in ministry. And while the now is important, the now changes quickly! Methods and materials change over time—principles do not. *The Red Book* is a tool that will hold up in an ever changing cultural landscape because it focuses on the "why." The deeper principles of ministry stay constant. Mark has captured so many key areas that are challenges in Children's Ministry. His years of experience and pastor's heart comes through so clearly. This is a invaluable book for children's ministry leaders young and old!

Spencer Click,
Executive Pastor & Ministry Coach

The
RED
Book

MARK HARPER

bush
PUBLISHING
& associates

The Red Book
Copyright © 2017 Mark Harper
ISBN: 978-1-944566-19-7

Bush Publishing & Associates books may be ordered at
www.BushPublishing.com or www.Amazon.com.
For further information, please contact:
Bush Publishing & Associates
www.BushPublishing.com

Contents

Introduction

T*he Red Book* is not about everything in children's ministry, but it is about the things that really matter.

The Red Book is about the things that don't change.

I have not written about culture and technology because the times are always changing, but the things that are most important are eternal—like God, they stay the same.

Children are precious to the Lord; that is why He called you to this ministry.

The focus of your ministry is kids, but in order to be successful as a kids' pastor, you have to know how to effectively communicate with parents and how to recruit and train volunteers. The lifeblood of any kids' ministry is volunteers. You can survive without money, but you can't survive without volunteers.

Additionally, it is vitally important that you maintain a good relationship with other leaders in your church. One of the dangers of children's ministry is that you can become isolated from the church body. This is not spiritually healthy for you or the children.

Not only does God want you to lead kids and peers, He also wants you to "lead up." In other words, it's important that you learn how to have influence with your senior pastor.

Finally, and most importantly, you are ministering to God when you minister to kids.

So, why *The Red Book*?

Red represents the blood of Christ. The blood of Christ is just as powerful in the 21st century as it was in the 1st century.

Think about the most important message that you can teach the kids in your class?

What would it be?

Most of us would agree that we need to teach our kids that Christ died for our sins and rose from the dead, and yet most kids' ministries shy away from a clear presentation of the Gospel.

It's amazing how many churches think a bold presentation of the Gospel is too strong for kids, but let's take a look at what God said to the Israelites concerning the Passover lamb in Exodus 12:3-8, 24-27 NIV:

> *Tell the whole community of Israel that on the tenth day of this month each man is to take a lamb for his family, one for each household. . . . Take care of them until the fourteenth day of the month, when all the members of the community of Israel must slaughter them at twilight. Then they are to take some of the blood and put it on the sides and tops of the doorframes of the houses where they eat the lambs.*
>
> *Obey these instructions as a lasting ordinance for you and your descendants. When you enter the land that the Lord will give you as he promised, observe this ceremony. And when your children ask you, "What does this ceremony mean to you?" then tell them, "It is the Passover sacrifice to the Lord, who passed over the houses of the Israelites in Egypt and spared our homes when he struck down the Egyptians." Then the people bowed down and worshiped.*

I hadn't seen this before, but recently I noticed that God instructs the children of Israel to select a lamb *four days* ahead of the Passover and to ***bring the lamb into their homes.***

I believe God did this so the family and the children would become attached to the lamb before the slaughter. He wanted kids and parents alike to feel emotion when they sacrificed the lamb—just a little bit of the pain that it cost the Father to sacrifice His Son.

This is not a pretty picture. I'm sure the kids were crying when the lambs were slaughtered. Then they had to take the blood of their lambs, and smear it on the doorpost of their houses. The children of Israel could not save their own kids. They needed the power of God to save their children.

For kids to have an understanding of the grace of God, they need to have an understanding of the price that Jesus paid for their sins.

My point is this: the Lord Jesus wants you to preach the deep things of the Word to the kids in your class.

Regardless of your denomination or church size, my prayer is that this book provides a strong foundation that you can build your kids' ministry upon.

Chapter 1

Begin with the End in Mind

Think about the kids in your class.

Get their faces in your mind.

Now imagine it is ten years in the future, and those same kids have graduated from high school.

How many kids in your current class will still be in your church when they turn eighteen?

How many will stay in church when they become adults?

Statistics show that 20 percent of the kids that grow up in church will stay in church when they become adults. Eighty percent leave the church they grew up in.

I don't think that eighty percent of our kids backslide. Many of them are attending other churches or have moved to other cities, but we can be more effective in keeping the kids that grow up in church.

When I first started in ministry, I could not think past the next service.

I would make it through Sunday morning, and I would think, *Whew, I made it.* But then I would wake up on Monday morning in a panic: *Oh, no! It's almost Wednesday!* I could never think past the next three days.

One Saturday night I was desperate. I was not ready for Sunday morning, so I was begging God for a new sermon idea, and I heard these words, "All you have is five years to prepare the kids for their teen years."

Young children are created with a nature to believe, but during their teen years, their faith will be challenged.

They will start to ask questions like:

- "Is God real?"

- "Is the Bible really the Word of God?"

- "Do I believe in God just because my parents do?"

Eventually, I began to think more long term.

For me "the end" is that the kids in children's church grow up in church and stay in church when they become adults.

I like what Dr. Phil says, "We are not raising kids. We are raising adults."

Here are some questions you need to ask:

- What can I do to prepare the kids for youth ministry?

- What do strong Christian fifth graders look like?

- What types of skills do they have?

Your list may differ from mine, but this is the list I came up with.

These are the skills I want my fifth graders to have:

1. Salvation

My kids have a real relationship with Christ. They are confident in their salvation experience. They remember the day they asked Jesus in their hearts.

2. Devotions

My kids have the ability to read the Bible for themselves and get something out of it. (Without this skill, they are doomed.)

3. Prayer

My kids have confidence in their prayer life. They know how to pray and get answers to their prayers.

4. Church

My kids attend church weekly because they want to.

5. Friends

My kids have strong Christian friends in the church.

6. Worship

My kids are passionate worshipers of Jesus Christ. They are not concerned about what their peers think.

7. Love

My kids experience the love of the Father and walk in love toward one another.

8. Holy Spirit

My kids know how to hear the voice of the Holy Spirit, and they want to obey Him.

9. Evangelism

My kids have a heart for the lost. They don't just focus on their friends at church, but they reach out to new kids. They know how to pray the prayer of salvation with a peer.

10. Leadership

My kids know how to think for themselves and make wise choices. They don't run to their parents for every decision.

11. Ministry

My kids are actively involved in ministry using their gifts in the church.

If this were where I want my fifth graders to be when they graduate to youth ministry, then I need to build my programs and my curriculum around these goals.

I realize that these are high goals for fifth graders, and I realize not every child will reach these goals; but please don't tell me it can't be done. I've seen too many kids that have graduated to youth with these skills to believe that it's impossible.

Get a vision for the kids in your class. See them accomplishing great things for God.

If you don't have a vision for them, then who will?

Chapter 2

Leading Children to Christ

"I tell you the truth, anyone who does not receive the Kingdom of God like a child will never enter it."

Mark 10:15

This scripture tells me that childhood is the time that God designed for us to receive the Gospel. Children have hearts that are sensitive to the Holy Spirit. They are created with natures to believe.

I love what Charles Haddon Spurgeon says in his book *Ministering to Children* about this scripture:

Say not, the child may not come till he is like a man, but know that you cannot come till you are like him. It is no difficulty in the child's way that he is not like you; the difficulty is with you, that you are not like the child. Instead of the child needing to wait until he grows up and becomes a man, it is the man who must grow down and become like a child.

Some people say that we should not try to influence kids to make a decision for Christ because kids are so easily influenced.

They reason, "Let the kids grow up, and then they can make a real decision that will last."

This is a huge mistake.

It's true that children are easily influenced. The truth is that kids are going to be influenced, so why not influence them for Christ?

I believe that God created children with soft hearts so that we could influence them with the Gospel.

We should present the Gospel on a regular basis to the kids in our class. Salvation is not the only subject we should teach, but it is the most important.

If a child receives Christ, make a big deal about it:

- Come up with a way you can celebrate their spiritual birthday with them.

- Create a book or handout to put in their hands immediately after they pray.

- Take some time to communicate with parents that their child received Christ.

Kids are so sensitive sometimes that they will come forward a second time to receive Christ, but I will only pray with them one time.

I ask them, "Have you asked Jesus in your heart before?" If they have already received Christ, I do not pray with them a second time. I confirm that they are already saved and that Jesus will never leave them. I want the kids in my class to be confident in their salvation experience.

Next time you see them, make sure to tell them that you are proud of them for making a commitment to Jesus Christ. Reaffirm their salvation experience every time you get the opportunity.

Chapter 3

How Come Kids Don't Read the Bible?

One of my stated goals is that the kids in my class have a regular time for devotions. After having a true salvation experience, this is number two on my list.

Let's face it; if they do not have a regular time of feeding on God's Word, they are not going to make it through their teen years.

One day I asked for a show of hands, "How many of you read the Bible or have your parents read it to you every day?"

Out of 200 kids in my class, 30 hands went up.

This was not good news.

When I am having an 85 percent-failure rate, I can't blame the kids; it's a leadership issue.

I asked myself some hard questions:

- How come kids don't read the Bible?
- What is stopping them?

The answer was incredibly simple.

Most kids don't read the Bible because they have never done it.

They know the Bible stories from children's church, and they have streamed all the Christian kids' programming, but many kids have never cracked open a Bible.

That day I realized I needed to build Bible reading into my kidmin program.

I know this is radical, but we also stopped telling Bible stories in kids' church and let the kids actually read the Bible during small group time.

I purchased 200 NIV Bibles for kids that were eight years old and up. (For six- and seven-year-olds, we purchased beginners' story Bibles. Many can't read yet, but they can follow along with the pictures.)

We have everyone sit in small group of eight to ten kids.

Each child reads one verse from the Bible as we go around the circle. (If one child has trouble reading, we let him or her pass.)

After reading the Bible story, we ask questions.

I tell my small-group leaders not to preach to the kids but to lead by asking questions such as, "What did you get out of this story?" or "Why did David run away from Saul?"

I want the kids to experience reading the Bible and having the Holy Spirit speak to them as they read it.

One thing that is critical to do with the Old Testament stories is to talk to kids about how the stories point us to Christ:

- When Adam and Eve sinned, God said to the serpent that one of Eve's descendants would bust his head. This was a prophecy that Jesus is coming, and He is going to bust the devil's head.

- When God said to Abraham to offer his son, Isaac, as a sacrifice, that is a picture of God the Father offering Jesus on the cross.

- When Moses told the children of Israel to put blood from a lamb on their doorposts, the blood of the lamb saved them just as the blood of the Lamb saves us.

- Jonah spent three days in the belly of a big fish, and Jesus spent three days in hell.

Ask this question each week: "How does this Bible story point us to Christ?"

This gives children an understanding that the Bible is a supernatural book.

Chapter 4

Simple Prayer

"Once Jesus was in a certain place praying. As he finished, one of his disciples came to him and said, 'Lord, teach us to pray.'"
Luke 11:1

Why did the disciples ask Jesus to teach them how to pray? They could see that Jesus was getting answers to His prayers, and they were not.

I am a believer in participatory learning.

Just telling kids they need to pray is not good enough.

I want my kids to know how to pray and get answers to their prayers.

New believers don't know automatically know how to pray. In fact, when we are first saved, our prayers are usually selfish and misguided. Others use their prayer time as an opportunity to complain to God about their problems. This is offensive to the Lord.

Prayer is so important that I spend several months every year teaching on prayer.

Four principles I teach kids about prayer:

1. **Prayer is simply talking to God and listening to God.**

   Talk to God like you talk to your best friend, and take time to listen.

   It's rare that God physically gives you the answer to your prayer. Most of the time, God will give you something to do that leads you to your answer.

   This is why it is so important to develop the skilling of listening when you pray. Don't do all the talking when you pray. Half of your prayer life should be spent listening.

2. **Our prayer lives are more effective if we connect with what God wants for our lives.**

   It's possible to talk God into things, like Israel talked God into letting them have a king, but our prayer lives are much more effective if we hook up with His will.

3. **The Bible teaches us about the will of God.**

   If we base our prayers on the Bible, we have confidence God will answer our prayers.

4. **There are many different kinds of prayers.**

   Here is a short list of the different kinds of prayers:
   - Prayer for salvation - Romans 10:9
   - Prayer for forgiveness - 1 John 1:9
   - Prayer of faith - Mark 11:23
   - Prayer of agreement - Mathew 18:19
   - Prayer of intercession - 1 Timothy 2:1

I follow this pattern when teaching kids how to pray:

1. Teach on prayer.

This happens during large group. The next three steps happen in small group.

2. Practice prayer.

If I teach on the prayer of intercession, I ask one of the kids to pray for someone they know that needs salvation.

If I teach on the prayer before the meal, I ask one of the kids to practice praying for the food.

3. Listen when you pray.

Ask for one minute, and then just be quiet. This helps them develop the skill of listening when they pray.

4. What did you hear?

Ask the kids to share what they heard. When you do this, it gives the kids confidence that God will speak to them. If you are unwilling to do this, then I question if you even believe that God will speak to kids.

5. Ask for testimonies.

Did anyone get a prayer answered recently?

I still remember the first time I got a prayer answered. There is nothing that excites a young believer more than an answered prayer.

Chapter 5

Assemble Together

My goal is that the kids in my class attend church on a weekly basis. The reason I say *weekly* is because discipleship is most effective with a weekly commitment. I understand that the tendency today is for families to attend church every other week, but the bottom line is that the kids that attend church on a weekly basis are stronger Christians.

I know that you cannot control how often a parent decides to come to church, but there are things that you can do to be proactive in this area.

1. Make it a stated goal.

You are not trying to guilt parents to come to church. You are simply stating an observation that kids that attend church weekly are stronger Christians.

I've heard people say something like this: "Don't make a big deal about weekly attendance because you will frustrate the kids who can't attend weekly."

While I understand what they are saying, I don't agree. If weekly attendance is one of your goals, then you need to communicate it with parents, or it will not happen.

2. **Teach the kids in your class about the importance of attending church on a weekly basis.**

3. **Make kids' church really fun.**

   Work hard to make learning the Word of God fun and exciting. One of your goals should be to get the kids to want to come back next week. If kids are bugging their parents to go to church, it's hard for the parents to say no.

4. **Create opportunities for kids to make friends at church.**

   I do this through small groups and special activities. Kids will want to go to church to connect with their friends.

   Have an ice-cream social (i.e., get-acquainted meeting) for parents of first graders to help their child transition into kids' church.

   At this meeting, share with parents your vision and goals for every child that graduates to youth ministry.

   Talk about how important weekly attendance is.

   You may not reach everyone, but this strategy is more effective than whining about how uncommitted the parents are.

Chapter 6

Helping Kids Make
Friends at Church

"Two people are better off than one, for they can help each other succeed. If one person falls, the other can reach out and help. But someone who falls alone is in real trouble."

Ecclesiastes 4:9,10

If kids do not make friends at church during the grade-school years, then they will not make the jump to youth ministry. Teenagers want to hang with their friends, so if they don't have friends at church, they won't hang out at church.

One of the best ways to insure that kids will not fall away during their teen years is to help them make friends at church.

You can't make kids be nice to one another, but you can create an environment that helps kids make friends by removing the obstacles to friendship. To do this, it's critical to understand the social dynamics of your group.

At my church, kids generally fall into one of three categories:

1. Kids that attend our Christian school

These kids already have their friends, so they don't really have a need for friends at church. This is a positive for the kids who are part of the school, but it is a negative for the kids who do not attend the church's school.

The Christian-school kids are not trying to be cliquey, but that is what happens. When these kids are at church, they are not trying to make new friends because they already have their friends.

To counter this tendency, I teach on friendship and the importance of being nice to the new kid. I also break up the cliques when we attend overnight events like camp.

2. Homeschooled kids

These are really good kids, but they don't always have as many social experiences as other kids. Sometimes they are behind socially.

To counter this, I provide extra activities for the homeschooled kids. Many of the homeschool moms are highly motivated to lead these activities.

I also pull on these kids for ministry, which in itself creates more social opportunities.

3. Kids that attend other schools

These kids usually don't have any friends when they start at our church.

I talk to these kids about being proactive in making friends. The Bible says, "If a man wants friends, let him show himself friendly" (see Prov. 18:24). Stop feeling sorry for yourself; look for someone who also doesn't have a buddy, and extend friendship.

Creating Friend-Making Environments

You cannot choose their friends for them, but you can create environments that will help them make friends.

1. Form small groups for kids.

One of the hardest decisions I ever made was to take thirty minutes out of my preaching and dedicate it to small-group ministry.

The primary reason I did this was that I noticed the bigger the church got, the less connected the kids were.

Church is not just about the relationship between the pastor and his sheep. The glue that holds the church together is the love we have for one another.

2. Create opportunities for kids to serve in ministry.

When kids get involved in a ministry, they are spending time with other kids who love the Lord and want to give of their time to help others.

The payback that my leadership kids get is the lifelong relationships they develop at worship rehearsal and drama practice.

3. Plan social activities for families.

I try to plan one social activity per month for families with grade-school children. Most of these are not drop-off events but rather opportunities where families can hang together.

Here is a list of the activities I have done:

- Sledding party
- Lock in
- Roller skating party
- Easter egg hunt
- Gym and swim night at the YMCA
- Vacation family adventure
- World's largest squirt-gun fight
- Summer camp
- Zoo trip
- The 100-foot banana split
- Hay ride and apple orchard trip
- Halloween alternative party
- Christmas party and gift exchange
- Video-game camp

Do not underestimate how important community building is for your kids. It is worth your time. You don't have to do this all by yourself. Find some motivated parents to organize your activities.

Chapter 7

How to Get Your Fifth-Grade Boys to Worship

The worship of children is precious to the Lord. He really likes it when children worship Him. In fact, the Bible calls it perfect praise (see Matt. 21:16 NKJV).

If the worship part of the service is for the Lord, what do you think He wants?

- Does He want it to be exciting?

- Does He want us to worship Him passionately?

- What does a really good worship service look like?

There are many different styles and ideas about worship, but the bottom line is a good worship service is when everybody is participating.

If the kids are not singing, then you need to start asking some questions.

I was having a conversation with a children's pastor, and I asked, "What is your biggest challenge right now?"

"I can't get my fifth-grade boys to enter into worship," she replied.

I asked her, "Are you doing motions with your worship songs?"

"Yes, we are."

"What do the fifth-grade boys think of the motions?"

"They think the motions are stupid."

At that point, someone else chimed in. "You just need to pray that they will get their hearts right, and then they will want to do the motions."

Whoa! Wait a minute. Where does it say in the Bible that your heart isn't right if you don't want to do the motions?

The key to corporate worship is participation, but worship isn't everybody doing the same thing at the same time.

If your fourth and fifth graders are participating in worship, they will influence the whole group.

What does a good worship service look like?

Ask the oldest kids in your class.

Fourth and fifth graders think that they are little teenagers, so I would take a look at what worship looks like in the youth ministry. That's where your kids are headed, so it's good to sing songs that will prepare them for youth.

Here are some basic tips for a good worship service:

1. **Have young worship leaders on the platform.**

   We use kids, teens, and adults in our worship team.

2. **Have male and female worship leaders.**

   If there are no men on the stage, the boys will not enter in.

3. **Practice, practice, practice.**

   If you are using videos, you still need to have a rehearsal. If it's not important to you, it won't be important to the kids.

4. **Drop the kiddie songs.**

   Use songs that they sing in youth or in the main sanctuary.

5. **Not all songs work with kids.**

   Use songs that have less words and simple choruses.

6. **All leaders and teachers in the room need to participate in worship.**

   If the teachers aren't worshiping, the kids won't.

7. **Do regular teachings on how to worship God.**

8. **Pride is the biggest hindrance for kids.**

   If they are concerned about what their friends are thinking, they won't enter in.

9. **Be transparent.**

   Talk about how you have had to overcome your own pride issues.

Chapter 8

Love Your Neighbor

*"Jesus replied: 'Love the Lord your God with all your heart
and with all your soul and with all your mind. This is the first
and greatest commandment. And the second is like it: Love
your neighbor as yourself.'"*

Matthew 22:37-39 NIV

Kids don't automatically know how to love their neighbors,
so we need to teach on it.

The first thing we need to do is to connect kids with their
heavenly Father. We are to forgive even as we have been for-
given. It's impossible to walk in the agape kind of love until we
have experienced the love that the Father has for us.

We tend to think of kids as innocent and kind, but sometimes
kids can be cruel and selfish, especially as they approach puberty.
There are times that kids will do things that make me proud but
then the following week say something that is really harsh.

When I see negative behavior in kids, it's not my job to
punish; rather I see it as an indicator that I need to teach on

walking in love. Then I trust the Holy Spirit inside them to bring correction.

Here are some negative tendencies that kids can have and how I counter them:

1. Punishing Words

Kids can be incredibly cruel at times, especially in groups. I counter this by teaching what the Apostle Paul said. "Let no corrupt communication proceed out of your mouth, but that which is good to the use of edifying, that it may minister grace unto the hearers" (Eph. 4:29 KJV). We should never use our words to punish someone but only to build them up.

2. Negative Thinking

This may seem hard, but it's not really difficult to pick out the kids that have low self-esteem. This is critical for two reasons. It's not what their heavenly Father thinks of them, and it's hard to love others if they don't even like themselves.

I counter this by going out of my way to say positive things to the kids that have low self-esteem.

Another way to counter it is to ask them to help you with something. This can communicate that you have confidence in them.

3. Blaming Others

Not always but many times blaming is an indicator of unforgiveness. To counter this, I teach on how Jesus not only died for my sins, He died for those who sinned against me. Jesus already paid the price for those who sinned against me. It's offensive to Him if I still try to make them pay.

4. Wanting More Things

One of the worst habits a child can develop is a sense of entitlement. This is the attitude that the world owes me simply because I exist. This habit is reinforced in American culture because we equate gift giving with love. Counter this by teaching the kids to be givers: "It is more blessed to give than to receive" (Acts 20:35 NIV).

You can encourage your kids to walk in love by publically praising the kids that you catch being kind. Make a big deal about it.

Chapter 9

Kids Don't Have a Junior Holy Spirit

When children receive Christ, the Holy Spirit comes to live inside of them.

Kids don't get a junior Holy Spirit. They get the same Holy Spirit that you and I get.

Why does the Holy Spirit come to live in us? To lead and to empower us for ministry.

If I could do my parenting all over again, I would spend less time teaching my kids to obey me and more time teaching them to hear the voice of the Holy Spirit.

The bottom line is it's good for kids to obey their parents, but it's better for them to obey the voice of the Holy Spirit. Their parents are not always with them, but the Holy Spirit is always there.

- Do you believe this?

- Do you believe that the Holy Spirit lives inside the kids that you teach?

- Do you believe that the Holy Spirit speaks to kids?

Then start acting like you believe it, and teach on the Holy Spirit. The following is how I teach on the Holy Spirit.

The Holy Spirit speaks in three ways:

1. The Bible

The primary way that God talks to us is through the Bible. Sometimes we are reading the Bible and a certain verse will stand out to us. When this happens, it's critical that we do whatever the Holy Spirit is telling us to do.

2. The Inward Witness

"The Spirit Himself bears witness with our spirit that we are children of God."

Romans 8:16 NKJV

The second way that God leads us is when the Holy Spirit bears witness with our spirit.

With the Inward Witness, you don't hear anything. It's a spiritual feeling that you have in your gut. It's a red light or a green light.

You may be watching a TV show and get a yucky feeling on the inside. That's the red light, the inward witness, telling you to turn it off or change the channel.

Sometimes you'll hear people say, "I've got peace about that." What they are saying is, "I have a green light; the inward witness is telling me to go for it."

Here is a great way to teach kids what the Inward Witness is so it's not so vague:

- Ask the kids to be quiet for about thirty seconds while you tell a story:

- Imagine that you are in the cafeteria and eating your lunch. Your friend doesn't have any dessert, so you decide to share your dessert with your friend.

- When you think about that, what does it feel like inside?

- Let the kids respond. Most will say, "It felt good."

- Ask them to close their eyes again, and tell a different story.

- You are on the computer with a friend, and he pulls up a scary part of a movie you're not allowed to see. He tells you to watch it with him because it's really cool. You tell yourself that it's okay just this one time; your parents won't find out. Plus, you could just close your eyes if it gets really bad.

- Think about that for a minute.

- What does it feel like?

- Allow the kids to respond. Most will say something like, "A yucky feeling."

At that point, I ask this question:

- "Do you need to ask your parents if it's wrong to disobey and watch the movie?"

- They always say, "No!"

- "Why not?"

- "We know on the inside that it's wrong to disobey."

- "See, that's the Inward Witness. You have the Inward Witness on the inside of you. You don't have to wait until you grow up to get the Inward Witness. This is how the Holy Spirit leads you. You can hear the voice of the Holy Spirit right now."

I want to give them confidence that they can hear the voice of the Holy Spirit.

3. Your Conscience

"Paul began: 'Brothers, I have always lived before God with a clear conscience!'"

Acts 23:1

If you are born again, your conscience is a safe guide. Your conscience is an inward voice. It's different from the Inward Witness because you actually hear words on the inside. The Bible calls it a still small voice.

I've taught kids to listen to the voice of their conscience by putting them in real-life situations. "How many of you have ever walked past your bedroom, and seeing it all messy, you heard a voice say, 'Remember, Mom told you to clean up your room'?"

That still small voice is your conscience, and it is one way that the Holy Spirit leads you.

Spiritual Exercise

To teach children about the still small voice, ask everyone to bow their heads and close their eyes.

- Tell them, "Listen to your heart."
- Wait about sixty seconds, and just listen.
- "Did anybody hear anything?"
- As children raise their hands, have them come forward and tell what they heard.

I do this exercise to give confidence to kids that they can hear the voice of the Holy Spirit.

Of course with kids, some of them will say silly stuff, but it's wonderful to hear some of the profound Holy Spirit-inspired things others will say. When one of them says something that's obviously inspired by the Spirit, I make a big deal about it.

Chapter 10

Can Kids Help Us Reach People for Christ?

I don't want to just teach on evangelism: I want the kids in my class to be practicing evangelism.

Many of our kids are great video-game evangelists. When they play a game that they like, they tell a friend. They use their influence to get their friends to purchase the game.

My point is that kids have a lot of influence with other kids. Why not leverage that influence for Christ?

I train the kids in my class to be evangelists in four ways:

1. Give them a heart for the lost.

This does not come naturally for kids who have grown up in church. Most church kids see lost people as the bad people—the kids that Mom doesn't want them to hang with. They really don't understand that there are billions of people in the world that do not know Christ.

I give kids this understanding in two ways: I teach on it, and I ask people that did not grow up in the church to share testimonies.

Storytelling is a great way for kids to connect with experiences that they have not had.

2. Be nice to the new kids.

They easiest way to evangelize is to "catch the fish in your own bathtub."

Teach your kids to be on the lookout for new kids. I tell the kids, "Don't clique out and just focus on your friends. If you see a new kid, go up and introduce yourself. Ask some questions."

We train our volunteers to do this. Why don't we train our kids? Think about it from the new kid's point of view. Do you want to make friends with an adult volunteer or another kid?

3. Have them invite friends to church.

This is something that kids love to do.

I find it is good to have several events during the year where our focus is evangelism. For me, that is Vacation Bible Adventure and our Halloween alternative.

I teach on evangelism for several weeks before VBA, and I give out a prize to the kid who brings the most friends. At VBA, I preach a salvation message and give an altar call. Kids love it when they see their friends respond to the altar call. Then they really start to catch the spirit of evangelism.

4. Teach the kids to pray the prayer of salvation.

The prayer of salvation is found in Romans 10:9: *"If you confess with your mouth that Jesus is Lord and believe in your heart that God raised him from the dead, you will be saved."*

There are two things that are included in this prayer:

- Believe in your heart that God raised Jesus from the dead.

- Say with your mouth that Jesus is Lord.

After teaching on it, I ask the kids to role-play and practice on each other. We keep doing it until every child knows how to pray this prayer. This gives them confidence that they can lead another child to Christ. I find the more confidence they have to pray this prayer, the more they will talk about Jesus to their friends.

Chapter 11

Let the Children Lead

Who has the most influence in your class?
(It may not be you. It might be one of your kids.)

In John Maxwell's book *The 5 Levels of Leadership*, he states that the lowest level of leadership is that people follow you because they have to.

The second level of leadership is that people follow you because they want to.

The person in authority is not always the strongest leader. It's very possible "Joey" is functioning at a higher level of leadership than you. In other words, your kids could be following you because they have to and following "Joey" because they want to.

When I turned fifty, I had to ask myself, "What does a fifty-year-old children's pastor look like?" I figured out that I don't have to be cool; I just have to have cool people around me. I leverage their coolness.

This is why I get kids and teens involved in my ministry—because they have more influence than I have.

If you want to move a group of people from point A to point B, you need to get the peer leaders on your side. The first thing you need to do is to identify your leaders, and then send everything through the leadership filter.

Who are your leaders? They are the oldest kids in the room. For me it was the fourth and fifth graders.

When we launched small groups for kids at my church, I noticed that it seemed to have a negative impact on our worship. Our kids were not entering into worship, and I couldn't figure out why. This went on for months, and then it dawned on me what was going on.

We had small groups organized by grade; so we had first graders on the front row, second graders on the second row, and so on. In other words, I had my leaders (fifth graders) on the back row. When it was time to worship, our first graders would run up to the front, but our fifth graders didn't want to go up there.

So I changed it. Now my fifth graders sit on the front row, and it totally changes our worship. If you target younger kids, you will lose the leaders. If you target your leaders, you will reach the whole group.

Chapter 12

Discovering Young Leaders

There are young leaders in your class. They may be the kids who are trying to take over.

Sometimes what we call *rebellion* is really young leaders trying to use their leadership gifts.

One thing about leaders is that they want to lead.

If they can't find a positive way to use their leadership, they will find a negative way to use their gift.

Here are six steps for developing leadership gifts in kids:

1. **Identify your leaders.**

   Who are the most popular kids in your class? (They currently have the most influence.)

2. **Give them something to do.**

   (There is a list of ministry jobs kids can do in Chapter 13.)

3. **Listen to your young leaders.**

   Do you like it when your pastor listens to you?

4. Affirm their ideas.

Nothing is more rewarding to a leader than when you take his or her idea and do it.

5. Teach them about servant leadership.

The biggest part of leadership is what happens at the back of the room.

6. Leading and following are connected.

Teach that if they want to lead, they need to follow first.

Chapter 13

What Is the Most Important Thing I Can Do to Make Sure My Kids Stay in Church When They Turn Eighteen?

When parents ask me, "What is the most important thing I can do to make sure my kids stay in church when they become adults?" I do not hesitate:

"Get them involved in ministry at a young age, and keep them involved."

It's true with every generation.

People that get involved in church stay in church.

People that do not get involved in church may hang around for a while, but they will eventually leave.

I had a unique opportunity to observe this firsthand. I was the kids' pastor at a mega church in Minneapolis from 1986 to 1992. Then I was in my own ministry for ten years before I was offered my former job again at the same church in 2002.

When I returned, I was looking for the kids that grew up in my children's church, but many of them were nowhere to be seen. The statistics held true. About 80 percent of my kids from the eighties were not at my church anymore.

On the bright side, I found that 60 percent of the kids that were involved in ministry in the eighties were still in the church.

Here are some examples:

- Monica was eleven when she started leading worship in Super Church (our children's ministry). Today Monica is thirty-five, and she sings in the sanctuary. She never left the church, and she has always used her gift for the Lord.

- Seth is the grade-school department head.

- Kelly is one of our youth pastors.

- Krista and Ginger teach in our Christian school.

- Jacob owns his own business, and he is one of the best teachers in Super Church.

All of them started in ministry at 9 or 10 years old. They were on the puppet team or the worship team or the AV team; and they are still in ministry today.

Jesus told us to go into all of the world and make disciples (see Matt. 28:19).

According to *Young's Concordance,* a "disciple" is a "taught or trained one." When the heart of a pastor is discipleship, that pastor gives people opportunities to do things. Likewise, a children's pastor gives kids opportunities to do things. If you are a one-man team, you are not making disciples.

They say that 20 percent of the people in our churches do 80 percent of the work. Why is that? Maybe it is because we tell them when they are children that they can't do anything for the Lord, and they continue to believe that when they become adults.

What are some things that kids can do in church? I'm glad you asked that question.

Here is a list of things that I have asked kids to do:

- Take up the offering
- Help new kids find a seat
- Help children get checked in
- Run sound or computer
- Pray for the sick
- Teach an object lesson
- Puppetry
- Drama
- Sing
- Play the piano
- Lead worship
- Run a camera
- Pray with kids for salvation
- Intercessory prayer

Kids can do whatever you will take the time to train them to do. Pick one child, and get started today.

Chapter 14

Feed My Lambs

"When they had finished eating, Jesus said to Simon Peter,
'Simon son of John, do you love me more than these?'
'Yes, Lord,' he said, 'you know that I love you.'
Jesus said, 'Feed my lambs.'"

John 21:15 NIV

One of the first things that the Lord Jesus asked Peter to do was "feed My lambs." Jesus saw qualities in Peter where He trusted him to feed the young ones in His flock.

There is a specific calling to feed the lambs.

What you do is very important to the Lord.

The preaching that you do on Sunday morning is the only meal that some of your kids are getting. This is why what you do is precious to the Lord.

Take a look at what Charles H. Spurgeon says in chapter one of his book *Come, My Children* about the Lord's instructions to Peter:

> *It is very remarkable that the word used here for "feed My lambs" is very different from the word employed in the precept "feed My sheep." I will not trouble you with Greek words, but the second "feed" means exercise the office of a shepherd, rule, regulate, lead, manage them, do all that a shepherd has to do towards a flock; but this first feed does not include all that it means distinctly feed, and it directs teachers to a duty which they may, perhaps, neglect—namely, that of instructing children in the faith. . . . Christian children mainly need to be taught the doctrine and life of the gospel: they require to have Divine truth put before them clearly and forcibly. Why should the higher doctrines, the doctrines of grace, be kept back from them? . . . Teach the little ones the whole truth and nothing but the truth; for instruction is the great want of the child's nature. A child has not only to live as you and I have, but also to grow; hence he has double need of food.*

Kids need more of God's Word and yet biblical illiteracy is at an all time high in America.

When I talk to professors at Bible colleges they tell me that new students seeking theological degrees know little to nothing about the Bible.

Is this a problem? It's more than a problem-it's a crisis.

Ironically, this digression has happened at a time where the church in the USA has spent hundreds of millions of dollars on themed classrooms, high-tech media centers, and full time KidMin pastors.

We have beautiful buildings and dedicated staff, but our kids are not learning the Bible. **This generation is spiritually**

starving to death. My question for you is do you want to be part of the problem or part of the solution?

The problem is clear;
kids are not learning the Bible.

In my opinion, too many of us have bought into the philosophy of "teach less for more." The good news is there is a solution for this crisis.

The Solution is: Teach More Bible.

If our kids are starving, the answer is more food, not less.

Peter finally did get understanding of his assignment from Christ. I know this because the first thing that Peter tells pastors to do is, "feed the flock of God."

As Children's Ministry Pastors, we have to think about many things including security, recruiting volunteers, dealing with angry parents and staying current with the culture. *At times, it can be overwhelming, but let's not lose sight of our number one job-feeding the sheep.*

Why do we need to read the Bible?

Christianity is a relationship with Jesus Christ, and the purest way to fellowship with Christ is to read His words. We need to get into the Words of Christ and get the Words of Christ into us. If we don't do that we will not make it.

Peter said it like this, *"Like newborn babies, you must crave pure spiritual milk so that you will grow into a full experience of salvation"* (1 Peter 2:2).

The Word of God is nourishment for our soul. Not only will we not grow up spiritually without the Word of God, we will not survive without it.

Here is why preaching to kids is so critical—more critical than any other ministry, in fact. ***Kids under the age of eight can't read yet. They are totally dependent on someone else to feed them.***

Don't parents have responsibility here? Absolutely, but you can't control what the parent's do. You can't control what the youth pastor does after you. You can only control what you do.

It's a great idea to hand out curriculum to parents so they can preach it at home, but you still can't make them preach to their kids.

One day I asked this question to the kids in my class.

"How many of you read the Bible every day or your parents read you the Bible every day?"

Out of 200 kids, only 40 hands went up. I was in shock. We did a great job of creating resources for parents at our church and still only 20% were using the resources.

The bottom line is this: many of the kids in your class are only getting one meal a week. The Word that you are preaching is precious to your kids and it's precious to the Lord.

You have your kids for one hour every week. Make sure you are doing your job and doing it well.

Feed the lambs.

Teach the Word and Go Deep! (If it's in the Bible you can preach it to kids.)

Teach in a way that holds their attention, don't just entertain them.

Preach the Word and preach it with passion.

Chapter 15

Feed Yourself

If you are going to feed the flock, you need to feed yourself.

- Never stand up in front of a group of kids and just read the curriculum.

- Be prepared.

- Preach out of your overflow.

If you are preaching on prayer, then look up scriptures on prayer and meditate on them. Find some good books on prayer, and read them during the week. The more time you spend in the Word of God, the better your preaching will be.

One of the side benefits of teaching kids is that you as an adult grow as you prepare to teach the kids. You learn more about God by reading the Bible for yourself than just listening to the preacher, but if you really want to grow by leaps and bounds, then make a commitment to teach a Sunday-school class. You really have to dig deep and study if you are going to teach the Bible to others.

Many curriculums today do not teach the deep things of the Word. The world is getting bolder with their message, yet the church seems to be more timid.

Jesus commands us to, "Preach the gospel to every creature" (Mark 16:15 KJV).

Kids have to fight the same devil that we have to fight. Children don't need less of God's Word today; they need more. Make sure you give them some meat and not just the dessert.

If it's in the Bible, you can preach it to kids, but preaching to kids is very different than preaching to adults.

Chapter 16

Ten Steps for Preaching to Kids

1. Focus on the bottom line.

What is the one thing you want your kids to do with the message you are preaching?

2. Think like a child.

If you are teaching on prayer, what types of things would a child pray for?

3. Teach in a series.

This will help your flock know where you are going.

4. Be visual.

Preaching to kids without something visual does not work. Always prepare an illustrated sermon that includes a short film, an object lesson, a game, a drama, or something similar, to provide a visual picture of your message takeaway.

5. Tell stories.

The best preachers are good storytellers. Many people (including children) learn by hearing stories. Stories take the truth you are teaching and apply it practically.

There is an art to storytelling, which means it's a skill you can develop. Look online for resources that can educate you on becoming a better storyteller. A master in the storytelling industry is Pixar™. Begin with searching for the rules Pixar™ follows to tell a great story, and start applying them to your illustrations this week.

6. Keep it moving.

One child who breaks the rules is a discipline problem. If the whole group is not paying attention, it's a leadership problem. Change what you are doing every five minutes or so. Don't change your message, but do change your method of delivery.

7. Stay current.

If you thought it was cool when you were growing up, it's not cool today. If you package an eternal message in an old wrapper, it will come off like an old message. How do you know what is cool? Ask your fifth-grade kids.

8. Target your peer leaders.

Your leaders are the oldest kids in the room.

9. Be funny.

When people laugh, it opens up their hearts. Use the sandwich method: Be funny. Preach the Gospel. Be funny.

10. Review and repeat.

Kids don't get it if you just say it one time. (Neither do adults.)

Chapter 17

A Time to Laugh

One of the great things about kids' ministry is all the funny stories. Sometimes the kids create the drama, and sometimes it's the kids' pastor.

Early in my ministry, I was doing a kids' crusade at Good Shepherd Assembly in Owensboro, Kentucky. We crammed eighty-five kids into the kitchen. The kids were all sitting on the floor because we didn't have room for the chairs.

I was teaching "How to Use the Word of God to Resist the Spirit of Fear."

I used apples to represent fearful thoughts (e.g., "Somebody is outside your window") and a machete to represent the sword of the Spirit, which is the Word of God.

I would throw apples (i.e., fearful thoughts) in the air and quote scripture: "Greater is He that is in me" and then slice the apple with the machete. It was a great sermon. The fifth grade boys loved it!

I had taught this lesson many times with great success; however, on this day with eighty-five kids crammed in a hot kitchen, I missed slicing the apple.

The kids thought it was hilarious, but I was embarrassed.

I tossed the apple in the air again, swung the machete, and missed a second time.

The kids were rolling on the floor laughing at my expense.

I was determined to be successful, so I threw the apple in the air a third time. I swung the machete with great intensity, and I sliced the apple right through the middle, but then everything switched to slow motion as the machete went flying out of my hand.

My heart skipped a few beats as I watched the point of the machete hit the carpet, bounce back up, and do a flip. I was powerless to stop it as I watched the handle of the machete land in the lap of a wide-eyed nine-year-old boy who was sitting in the front row on the floor.

The brave lad looked up at me and said, "I'm not afraid! I'm not afraid!"

He thought it was part of the lesson.

What did I learn from that experience?

Learn to laugh at yourself.

Chapter 18

What Type of Kids' Pastor Are You?

There are different types of kids' pastors. This is why it can be dangerous to go look at someone else's program and copy it. If a church has a successful program, then they built their program around the strengths of the leader; but you may or may not have those same strengths.

I'm not saying we shouldn't learn from others. Everyone needs a mentor or two, but to totally copy someone else's ministry is a mistake.

> *You need to build your kids' ministry around your strengths.*

This means you need to know what your strengths are, and you need to know what your weaknesses are. You need to look for people to help you who are strong in areas that you are weak.

Your strengths are things that you enjoy doing that bring you fulfillment.

Ask yourself the following questions:

- Are you more of a visionary or a detail person?

- Are you task orientated or people orientated?

- Do you like to lead from the front of the room or the back of the room?

- What brings you the most fulfillment: working with kids, parents, or volunteers?

It's rare to find a church that is strong in all three areas.

I have seen children's programs that are well organized. Their systems are in place, but the actual kids' ministry is not very good. This leader is someone who is great at administration but may not have a strong teaching gift.

I have also observed children's programs that have a good program for the kids, but it's not very organized. In this situation there is usually one person, the kids' pastor, who is very good with the kids, but there is no one leading from the back of the room. Volunteers do not hang around because no one is ministering to them.

In the last decade, there has been a shift toward family ministry with a focus on ministry to kids through their parents. This can be a positive thing, but I have seen some of these churches drop the ball in their kids' ministry on Sunday mornings.

Is it possible to be good in all three areas?

Absolutely, but you can't do it by yourself. It begins with you deciding what part you want to do. I love the following quote from American actor Ben Stein: *"The indispensible first step to getting what you want out of life is this: Decide what you want."*

- Do you want to be the primary teacher of the kids?

- Do you enjoy the recruiting, training, and organizing of the volunteers?

- Do you want to focus on ministering to the kids through their parents?

Decide what you want to do, but that does not excuse you from the things you don't want to do. They are still your responsibility. You will need to find people that can help you in the other areas.

Chapter 19

Are You at the Right Church?

This should be super obvious, but it's amazing how many kids' pastors get tripped up because they are not at the right churches.

If you are called to minister to kids, you are called to do it through a local church.

A successful kids' ministry costs money and requires volunteers, perhaps more volunteers than any other ministry in the church. You need the help and resources that a local church can provide.

There will be times in your ministry journey where your commitment to your church is tested. If this hasn't happened yet, trust me, it will. You need to be prepared for the temptation to quit.

But if you quit, the team just gets weaker.

Most of you reading this have a church home, but there may be opportunities on your journey where you are looking for a church to connect to.

Here are some questions to ask when choosing a church to serve in:

- Am I in agreement with the church doctrine?

- Does the senior pastor's preaching feed me?

- Can I hook up with the vision of the church?

- Do I understand how the church is governed and how decisions are made?

- Do I like the senior pastor?

- Do I like the worship, and am I in agreement with the style of the worship?

- Would I attend here if I weren't getting paid?

If you can't answer yes to all of these questions, my suggestion is to keep looking until you find a church where you believe you can spend the rest of your life. Kids' ministry can be stressful, but if you know you are where you are supposed to be, it reduces a lot of the stress.

> *"He makes the whole body fit together perfectly. As each part does its own special work, it helps the other parts grow, so that the whole body is healthy and growing and full of love."*
> Ephesians 4:16

You have a special work to do.

You want to make sure you are offering your supply at a church where you will be most effective.

Chapter 20

Building Your Team

"Follow me and I will make you fishers of men."
Matthew 4:19 KJV

What was Jesus doing when He said these infamous words? He was building His team.

"You did not choose Me, but I chose you."
John 15:16 NKJV

This tells me that Jesus was selective about who was on His team.

What kind of people was Jesus looking for? He was looking for leaders.

That's why the disciples were fighting all the time. They all wanted to be the leader.

He could have said it like this: *"Follow Me, and I will make you a leader."*

Always be on the outlook for new leaders.

What are you looking for when you are building your team?

You are not looking for followers at this point. You are looking for leaders.

It's one thing to lead followers and another thing to lead leaders. Followers are people who want to follow. They don't really want to make decisions.

Leaders are people who want to lead. They have opinions that are different than yours.

I love this quote by Andy Stanley: "If you are a leader and leaders work for you, they think they can do a better job than you. They just do. (Just like you do.) And that's not wrong; that's just leadership."

That kind of says it all right there. Take a look at your current volunteers, and start building your leadership team.

Here are five steps to building your leadership team:

1. Staff to your weakness.

Look for people who are strong where you are weak. If you are not good with details, surround yourself with people that are good with details. If you are a woman, get some men on your team.

Sometimes people will say things like, "I'm not good at drama, so we don't do drama skits." If you are not good at something, it is an opportunity to add another leader.

2. Identify your leadership positions.

Write down a list of all your leadership positions.

This is my list. It's not a complete list, but you get the idea. Your list is going to look different than mine.

- Nursery Director
- Pre-School Director

- Worship Leader
- Drama Director
- Small-Group Director
- Volunteer Specialist
- Lead Teachers – 4
- Head Coaches – 3
- Small Group Leaders – 30
- Small Group Assistants – 30

3. See yourself as a resource to your leaders.

I will never forget when I shared the idea with my pastor for creating the Super Church curriculum.

He looked at me and said, "One of my jobs as pastor is to be a resource to you, to help you fulfill your vision."

I could not believe what I was hearing. I had never heard a pastor talk like that. Didn't he hire me to help him?

Yes, your leaders are there to help you, but you are also there to help them.

The more you help grow your leaders, the more they will help you. You help yourself when you help others. It's a spiritual law: do unto others what you would have them do unto you (see Luke 6:31).

4. Schedule regular brainstorm meetings.

Start meeting on a regular basis with your leaders, at least once a month. I like meeting with all my leaders at a local cafe for a brainstorming session.

I already know all of my ideas. The purpose of a brainstorming meeting is to listen to their ideas and to create some synergy. When someone shares a good idea, I put it into action. It is really motivating to leaders when you take one of their ideas and run with it.

This is my favorite part of the ministry. I love to dream and create with a team.

- I draw energy from the team.

- God has big plans for your ministry.

- Don't try to do it all by yourself.

- The best way to grow your ministry is to add leaders to your team.

There are leaders in your church who want to help you lead; they just need to be asked.

5. Invest in your leaders.

The more you invest in your leaders, the more you will get out of them. One of the best ways to invest into your leaders is to take them to a conference. Many people do their training online today, but you can't get that group experience online.

Chapter 21

Leading Leaders

It's one thing to lead followers and another thing to lead leaders. How do I get people to follow me who would rather be the leader, and why should I try to get people to follow me who don't really want to follow?

Followers are great at getting things done, but you will reach more people if you focus your time and energy on leading leaders. There are risks in trying to lead leaders, but if you try to do it all by yourself, then you are guaranteed to fail. If you want to grow as a leader, you have to increase your influence with other leaders.

Here are three important steps in leading leaders.

1. Be quick to hear.

Create environments where you take time to listen to your leaders. You can do this one-on-one, but I like to do it as a group.

2. Be slow to speak.

If you want to lead leaders, then you will have to do more listening and less talking. If you put someone in charge of a meeting, never jump in the middle of it. You can probably communicate it better, but that doesn't mean that you should.

It is really empowering to a leader when you can sit in the meeting and keep your mouth shut. It reinforces their leadership and communicates to everyone else that you trust them.

3. Be slow to wrath.

Your leaders will do things that provoke your anger. You may need to talk to them, but wait until you calm down. Nobody likes to be yelled at, especially volunteers. Sometimes one angry outburst can destroy a relationship.

If you follow this scripture, you will be well on your way to leading leaders: "Everyone should be quick to listen, slow to speak, and slow to become angry" (James 1:19 NIV).

Chapter 22

Loyalty

Let's talk about loyalty for a minute.

Loyalty is the glue that holds your team together. If you want loyalty from your leaders, be loyal to them.

I remember the first time I complained about another staff member to my pastor. He looked at me and asked, "Have you talked to them?"

"No."

"Then why are you talking to me?"

I never did that again.

From that point on, if I had a conflict with someone, I did what Mathew 18:15 NIV tells us to do: "If your brother or sister sins against you, go and point out their fault, just between the two of you. If they listen to you, you have won them over."

Have you been on the other side of that?

An angry parent complains about you to your supervisor, or another staff person tries to pull the "end run." If you have not had this experience yet, you will. The enemy does not want your team to bond together. He is going to take shots at you and your leaders.

Do you have a plan?

What do you do when someone complains to you about one of your leaders?

It's pretty simple really. Do what the Bible says: "Do to others as you would have them do to you" (Luke 6:31 NIV).

What do you want your team members to do when someone criticizes you? What kind of seeds do you want to sow? What kind of example do you want to set?

If you sow seeds of loyalty, your leaders will be loyal to you. If you are not loyal to your leaders, they will find someone else to follow.

Some of you may be thinking that your supervisor is not loyal to you. You may work at a church where the "end run" is part of the church culture. It seems like everybody does it.

- You cannot control what your boss does.
- You cannot control what anyone else does.
- You can only control what you do.

David practiced loyalty. He remained loyal to Saul even though Saul was not loyal to him.

Do you want to be a Saul, or do you want to be a David?

If you are loyal to your leaders, they will be loyal to you. It's similar to the principle of forgiveness. God doesn't tell me to forgive because He is taking the other guy's side. He tells me to forgive because it is good for me.

When you are loyal to your leaders that are on your team, it is good for you, it's good for them, and it's good for the kids in your church.

Whenever you promote people to new leadership positions, there are going to be people who challenge their leadership. Some people will think, *Why is that person in charge?*

Many years ago at kids' camp I had to miss a puppet rehearsal, so I put Kevin, who was fourteen, in charge of the rehearsal.

When I returned several hours later, Kevin was in tears. We had a total leadership meltdown, and service was going to start in one hour. I gathered Kevin and the rest of the team and corrected the whole team.

"If I put someone in charge, you need to listen to him like you listen to me."

I put Kevin in charge again, and we rehearsed all the skits one more time. (If a new leader fails, the worst thing you can do is take the leadership away from him.) After that experience, Kevin was totally committed to me, and he became one of my strongest leaders.

Do not put people in positions of leadership if you are not willing to back them up. They will get shot at. Your job is to cover their backs. If you've got their backs, they will have your back.

Is it possible that one of your leaders will be disloyal to you even if you are loyal to them?

Yes, it does happen; however, it's guaranteed that they will be disloyal to you if you are not loyal to them.

Chapter 23

Magnify Your Ministry

If you have been doing kids' ministry for any length of time, you have discovered that many do not see it as "real ministry." This is false, of course, but people's attitudes can still wear you down.

As the leader, it's critical that you not allow this to happen. You have to continue to encourage yourself. Here is a scripture that helped me:

> "I am speaking to you who are Gentiles. Inasmuch then as I am an apostle of Gentiles, I magnify my ministry."
> Romans 11:13 NASB

Paul said, "I magnify my ministry." He magnified his calling. Why did Paul have to magnify his ministry? Because some people in the church did not respect his ministry.

Paul was the apostle to the Gentiles. The Gentiles felt like second-class citizens in the book of Acts. Peter and James saw the Gentiles as a lesser ministry, but Paul did not see it that way. Father God didn't see it that way either. Christ died for both the Jews and the Gentiles.

There will be people in the church who see kids' ministry as a lesser ministry, but Father God does not see it that way. Kids' ministry is precious to our Heavenly Father.

Is kids' ministry more important than other ministries?

No, but it is a special work to the Lord.

Here's how I know:

There are many names for God in the Bible: Creator, El Shaddai, Jehovah Jireh, and many more; but the name He likes best is Father.

How do I know?

Because that is what Jesus called him—Father—and you can't be a father without kids.

Father God is the One that called you. He is the One that gave you this assignment, and ultimately you are doing it for Him.

There will be times it will seem like nobody cares about what you do. Your pastor may be clueless as to how much work you do; parents may be angry with you; volunteers may not show up; and staff members may disrespect you; but know that Father God is pleased with you.

If you are feeling disrespected, just remember that Paul was disrespected too. What should you do if someone disrespects you? Do what Paul did. Don't let it get you down; magnify your ministry.

- Kids' ministry is a call from the Lord.

- Don't ever feel sorry for yourself.

- Don't compare your ministry to other ministries in the church.

- Don't get defensive.

Magnify your calling.

People respond to passion. When you are passionate about kids' ministry, your fire will rub off on other people, and they will change.

Chapter 24

Five Essential Leadership Skills for Kids' Pastors

As you minister to the kids, you will grow as a leader. You are going to need a lot of volunteers to reach a lot of kids, so it's critical that you understand leadership and that you grow in your leadership skills.

Here is my list of the top-five leadership skills you need for kids' ministry:

1. Be an example.

The leader is the one who sets the pace. Peter said it like this:

Care for the flock that God has entrusted to you. Watch over it willingly, not grudgingly—not for what you will get out of it, but because you are eager to serve God. Don't lord it over the people assigned to your care, but lead them by your own good example.

1 Peter 5:2,3

Lead by your own good example.

You need to be the one who is more committed than anyone else. Don't just be on time for your volunteer meetings, be ten-minutes early.

Be prepared when you minister. Don't just get up in front of the kids and wing it. Don't ever just read the curriculum. The Scripture says to study to show yourself approved (see 2 Tim. 2:15). Preach out of your overflow.

Practice your drama skits. Memorize your lines. Test all your media elements on the screen before church so you are not embarrassed.

You are the leader. The kids are watching you. Your volunteers are watching you. They are only going to do what you do.

2. Be proactive.

When I first started in kids' ministry, I saw myself as a victim. I loved the kids, but I felt like my ministry was totally at the mercy of other people.

I played the blame game a lot:

Things would get better if . . .

. . . parents placed a higher value on their children.

. . . more people would step up and volunteer.

. . . my pastor understood how important kids' ministry is.

This type of thinking does not get you anywhere.

You do need people to help you minister to the kids, but people will not follow you just because you think they should.

A proactive person does not focus on the things he can't control. Don't waste time getting angry about things you can't control.

What are some areas that you do have control over?

• Your Thoughts

You have total control over your thoughts. Think about what you are thinking about. Are you constantly thinking negative thoughts about yourself?

I had a huge battle in this area because I grew up in a negative environment.

Choose to hang out with people who are positive and make you feel good about yourself.

• Your Words

Words are powerful. You can use your words to build people up or to tear people down.

People do not respond to guilt. They respond to passion. If you are excited about kids' ministry, people will want to follow you.

• The Kids

You are the person who has the most influence over the kid-min program.

Quit whining about people that don't see your vision. Make the children's ministry the most exciting ministry in the church. Only you can do this. Nobody is going to do it for you.

One day my pastor announced in a staff meeting that he had booked a special speaker for a New Year's Eve service. The service was starting at 8:00 p.m. and going until midnight. I was not happy about having to plan a four-hour kids' service in the middle of the holidays.

My first thought was self-pity, which then led to anger. After I got over my pity party, I got a great idea. What if I planned a New Year's Eve lock in for the kids? I had to be at church anyway, right?

I ran the idea by my pastor, and he liked it. Instead of trying to babysit the kids for four hours, we planned a big party.

Parents dropped off their kids at church at 8:00 p.m. At 10:00 p.m., we loaded up on a bus and took the kids to Chuck E. Cheese. We had all the pizza they could eat, all the pop they could drink, and all the video games were free. At 2:00 a.m., we reloaded the buses and went back to church for a lip-sync contest. Eventually, the kids rolled out their sleeping bags. Kids, parents, and volunteers all had a blast; so we made it an annual event.

A successful kids' pastor is proactive.

You don't have time for a pity party. Stop thinking about all the things you can't control, and pour your energy into the things you can control.

3. Vision Casting and Goal Setting

All leaders are visionaries. While vision casting and goal setting are not the same—they are connected.

Vision is simply the desired future. What do you see?

As believers in Christ, vision is not just something we imagine. It's something that comes from heaven. We want to be able to say with the Apostle Paul, "I was not disobedient to the vision from heaven" (Acts 26:19 NIV).

Proverbs 29:18 KJV says, "Where there is no vision, the people perish."

Churches need to have a vision for their kids, or their kids will perish. We will lose the next generation! This is why vision is so important.

Goal Setting is a way to measure progress toward what you see in the future, not just for you—for your entire team. Goal setting is important because it is highly motivating for your team to set some goals and then accomplish those goals. Unlike anything else, this gives your team confidence in your leadership.

Here is how I cast vision with my team:

- I have one meeting every year specifically for vision casting.

- I do this on a Saturday morning in January.

- Before I cast the vision for the coming year, we look at the vision from the year before and measure our progress. (I don't always accomplish every goal on the list, but I do accomplish most of them.)

- I cast the vision for that year illustrated with a Power-Point™ presentation.

This communicates to everyone that we do what we say we are going to do, and it creates momentum.

4. Delegate, Delegate, Delegate

To survive in kids' ministry, you need to learn the leadership skill of delegation.

As the kids' pastor, you have responsibility for ministry in multiple classrooms happening simultaneously, plus ministry to parents and first-time visitors, overseeing volunteers, and the constant need to recruit new volunteers. To make matters worse, all this is happening at the same time—on Sunday morning.

If this sounds stressful, it is; but only if you do it by yourself. The solution to this dilemma is to spread your leadership around by delegating to others.

For example, if you enjoy teaching first through fifth graders, you need to find good people to greet new parents, process check-in, oversee your volunteers, and teach the other classes.

Figure out what you are good at, and delegate the rest. You don't have to be good at everything. There are people in your church who are good at the things you are not.

My pastor says, "Delegate everything you can delegate." The more you delegate, the more it frees you up to be creative, and it gets someone else connected. It also communicates to your leaders that you trust them.

Do not hesitate to ask people to do the things you can't or don't have time for. This is the only way it may get done.

- **Don't be afraid of *no*.**
In the past, I have not asked people to do things out of the fear of rejection. Hey, the worst they can say is no. If they say no, you haven't lost anything. If you don't ask; however, you will never hear *yes*.

- **Don't make decisions for people.**
Some of my volunteers are stay-at-home moms. At times, I have felt guilty asking them to volunteer when I know they have many kids at home. I assumed that they didn't have time to volunteer, but I learned not to make the decision for them. Your volunteers are big people. If they can't do it, they will let you know.

- **Delegation is not dumping.**
There is a difference between delegation and dumping. When you dump, you ask someone to do something and then never talk to him or her again. You assume it is done.

Delegation is not just getting through your to-do list. It is mentoring people. You need to stay in regular communication with people that you delegate to.

5. Communication

I spend a lot of my time communicating with people. It just comes with the territory. That's why it's critical to take the responsibility to communicate with your leaders, volunteers, and parents.

Let people know what is expected of them up front, and follow through. Before each weekend, I communicate with everyone on the schedule. I usually communicate by e-mail, but sometimes I call people if it is really important. I have found that my teenage volunteers don't use e-mail. The best way to communicate with young people is by text or Facebook™.

My point is that people communicate in different ways, but I take the responsibility to make sure communication happens. For example, I don't assume that communication happens just because I fired off an e-mail. If I don't get a reply, then call to talk about the weekend.

Shouldn't my volunteers be more responsible than that? Maybe, but they are volunteers. They don't have to be there. Bottom line is I have less no-shows if I connect with people during the week. It also gives me an opportunity to speak into their lives.

Communication is a two-way street. It's not only about what you have to say. Real communication happens when you understand each other, so build listening into your communication.

Chapter 25

The Seven Deadly Sins of Kidmin Pastors

The call to pastor kids is an assignment from the Lord; however, the enemy does not want you to fulfill your assignment. He is going to set some traps to stop you or, at least, to slow you down. The good news is he doesn't have any new temptations. I have identified what I like to call the seven deadly sins of kidmin pastors.

In the spirit of transparency, the reason I know so much about these seven deadly sins is that I have participated in all of them. If you haven't been tripped up by one of these yet, you will in the future. We all deal with the same stuff no matter the size of our church or our denomination.

1. Isolation

Starting off the list is isolation. One of the challenging parts of kids' ministry is that you are separated from the rest of church. If you find yourself thinking, "Nobody else cares about the kids' ministry"; you are dealing with this sin.

You can't carry the load by yourself. The cure for isolation is to serve in some other ministries in the church. It's counterintuitive, but it's the only way to deal with it.

2. Narcissism

If truth were told, we all deal with this, but some of us have it worse than others. The narcissistic kids' pastor needs to be the center of attention. He or she loves kids but is unwilling to spread the love around.

Many times these kids' pastors are talented and really good at what they do, but they either don't know how to train someone else or they are unwilling.

If you find yourself changing churches every two to three years, this may be why.

The cure for the sin of narcissism is to start leading from the back of the room where no one can see you.

3. Jealousy

This green monster (and I'm not talking about the Hulk) can kill you. It goes something like this: You attend the latest, big conference, or you visit the local mega church that has a reputation for great kids' ministry.

The first thing you notice is how much money they have to spend. You want to ask how big their budget is, but you are too embarrassed. You immediately start to think about how much better you would be if you had a lot more money.

This, in turn, leads to anger that's directed at your pastor or elder board. The cure for the sin of jealousy is to forget about it.

Stop comparing yourself to other churches. Kids in America don't need more stuff anyway. Kids need someone who loves them and will be there for them, and you can do that for free.

4. Anger

Do you find yourself playing the blame game a lot? It's hard to be angry and happy at the same time.

If you aren't happy, you will end up quitting; and if you quit, the team gets weaker.

The cure for anger is to stop getting angry about things you can't control. Be proactive. Focus on the things you can control.

5. Self-Neglect

We are all familiar with child neglect, but what about self-neglect? It's easy to become a workaholic in ministry because the need is so great.

You can get emotionally addicted to the good feeling that comes from helping other people yet neglect yourself and those that you love the most.

Do you consistently work more than fifty hours per week?

Are you eating right, getting enough sleep, and exercising? Do you pray and read the Bible?

Do you attend church when you are not serving? If not, you won't last long.

Do you spend dedicated time with your spouse and kids? If not, your marriage won't last. Don't sacrifice your family for the ministry. It's not worth it.

The cure for self-neglect is to establish healthy boundaries and then follow through. Turn off your smart phone. Go off the grid. Focus dedicated time with those you love the most.

6. Laziness

Laziness and its evil twin *Procrastination* are huge problems. Some people are workaholics, but others are lazy.

Personally, I think laziness is a bigger problem today. Are you always waiting until Saturday to prepare for Sunday?

Procrastination will negatively impact the quality of your ministry. How much time do you spend in preparation for your sermons, or do you just like to wing it? Do you read books?

Many times in my mentoring groups, I will recommend good books to young leaders. I am shocked at how many will say to me, "I don't like to read." If you don't like to read, I'm okay with that, just find another career. Don't pursue ministry if you are too lazy to read a book.

The cure for laziness is simple—**Do the work**.

7. Bridge Burning

We all know that arson is a crime, but it's amazing how many people in ministry get a thrill out of burning bridges.

Don't quit your job if you are mad. Deal with your anger first.

Once you make the decision to leave, don't check out. Do everything in your power to make the transition smooth for the next guy.

After you leave, people will call, text, or message you and complain about the new guy. Don't listen to them. The new guy is going to do things differently than you, but it's not your problem. Encourage them to support their church and the new guy.

The cure for the temptation to burn your bridges is to finish strong. Work hard, and be nice to all people, especially at the end. You will be glad you did in a year or two.

The question is not are you going to fall into one of these sins? You will.

The question is: do you learn from your failures or do you just keep doing them?

Chapter 26

Boundaries in Ministry

Without question, the biggest challenge in ministry is creating healthy boundaries. Church, spouse, children, job, and friends all seem to blend together.

A boundary defines where you end and someone else begins.

Ask yourself these questions:

- Do you have trouble saying no?
- Do you have a regular day off?
- Do you get angry when other people tell you no?

The most basic boundary word is the word *no*. The demands of ministry are never-ending. If you are going to be in the race for the long haul, you need to know how and when to say no.

When I first started in ministry, I did not know how to say no. I was working every day and putting in seventy hours per week. I was telling myself that I was working for the Lord so it was okay.

Let's think about that idea for a minute. Does God really want me working seventy hours per week? Wasn't He the One who created the concept of a day off every week?

The truth is that if you establish healthy boundaries in your ministry, you will reach more people and enjoy your life more.

Here are some tips for creating healthy boundaries in ministry:

1. Fight for your day off.

Establish at least one day every week for you and your family. Do not go to church on this day. Do not read your e-mails. Do not think about work. Have some fun!

2. Listen to your spouse.

Debbie and I have always been a ministry team. This has its advantages and disadvantages. One of the disadvantages is that we are always talking about the ministry. We have this agreement that if one of us says, "I don't want to talk about ministry right now," then we change the subject.

3. Create a not-to-do list on a weekly basis.

When you write out your to-do list, also create a not-to-do list. If you going to do something new, you will have to give up something you are currently doing.

4. Learn how to say no to your boss.

I had a really hard time saying no to my pastor because I wanted to please him. I think most of us feel this way. So if my pastor asked me to do something new and I had the time to do it, I would say yes.

If it made me feel overwhelmed, I would respond by saying something like, "This week I am working on project A. I can take on the new project, but I will have to put off project A. Which one do you want me to work on?"

This is much better than saying, "No, I don't have the time," because it gives my pastor the steering wheel. If my pastor wants me to change course and work on something new, it's no sweat off of my nose because I serve him.

Ministry is a marathon, not a sprint. Keep running your race.

If you are constantly feeling overwhelmed, it may mean it's time to create some boundaries.

Chapter 27

The Lifeblood of Kids' Ministry

Volunteers are the lifeblood of any kidmin program.

I can survive without money, but I cannot survive without volunteers.

When I began in kids' ministry, I was all about the kids. I was young and full of energy, so I threw all my passions into the kids. I viewed volunteers as people who were assisting me so I could teach the kids.

I know this seems harsh, but there were times when a volunteer might approach me with a problem, and I viewed it as a distraction from my ministry to the kids. The Holy Spirit would whisper to me, "This is ministry too."

See, it's all part of your ministry because you belong to Christ; and Christ died for your kids, your volunteers, the parents, and even your pastor.

As I matured as a leader, my thinking began to change. I still love preaching to kids, but I get more fulfillment out of training others to preach to kids. I call it "double-dipping." The kids get ministered to and the volunteer grows at the same time.

When you train others to do what you do, everybody wins.

What do volunteers want?

Before recruiting any volunteers and telling them what *you* want, ask yourself this question: what do *volunteers* want?

They want to be part of a cause because it feels really good to give of their time to help someone else. People want to volunteer.

The reality is that people only have so much time to give.

I like to look at the volunteer as my customer, so I ask, "What does my customer want?" You will have more success in recruiting and keeping your volunteers if you look at things from their perspective first.

Here is a list of eight things that all volunteers want:

1. **Volunteers want you to be prepared for them.**

   As the leader, my job is to equip my volunteers so they can focus on the kids. I used to look at it like it was their job to help me so I could minister to the kids. As you can imagine, my volunteers didn't hang around very long. This means that I do the sermon prep and purchase the supplies so all they have to do is study the lesson and show up on time. I want my volunteers thinking about the kids.

2. **Volunteers want to be greeted.**

   This is especially important on the first day. Know their names, and be excited to see them. Let your other leaders know that a newbie is showing up so everyone is prepared to greet them.

3. **Volunteers want good training.**

   Don't just throw them to the wolves. Make sure your new recruits have someone to mentor them. Some of my volunteers are good at teaching kids but not at mentoring other teachers. I put my new volunteers with someone that has a heart for mentoring others.

4. Volunteers want you to respect their time.

Start and end your meetings on time.

5. Volunteers want to be appreciated.

Give a heartfelt *thank you* to your volunteers, but more importantly catch them doing something right. Give genuine praise when you see someone go the extra mile. The Lord notices the little things that volunteers do, and you should too.

6. Volunteers want you to communicate with them.

Regular communication is motivating for volunteers, while the lack of it is one reason volunteers become dissatisfied. Volunteers like to have one person who mentors them. You will lose any volunteers who are not looked after.

7. Volunteers want to be heard.

They may not want to be the decision makers, but they do want someone to listen to their ideas. Build time into your training for listening. It is incredibly motivating to volunteers when you use one of their ideas.

8. Volunteers want to be connected.

People are looking for community—that place where they feel loved and accepted. In fact, building community is the most important thing you can do to keep volunteers for the long haul.

Chapter 28

Building Community

The other day I bumped into a friend at Starbucks. My friend was overseeing the kidmin program at a new church, and he asked if I could meet with him sometime. Then he made this statement: "We are burning through a lot of volunteers."

If you are burning through volunteers, then your volunteers are not having pleasant experiences.

Learn how to build a community. Create an atmosphere where people want to hang out in kids' ministry. If your volunteers are learning, having fun, and feeling like they are contributing, they will hang around.

Many years ago, I asked my good friend Jim Wideman if I could follow him around on a Sunday morning. I was hurting for volunteers, and Jim has a reputation for being the volunteer guru. I thought I could learn something by just tagging along and watching him.

To my surprise, what Jim did was incredibly simple. He just walked around and talked with people. If you know Jim, you know that he is a hard worker. He might even be a workaholic, but he wasn't doing work on Sunday morning. He was just talking to people about Alabama football and good barbeque.

What Jim does best is make people feel good about themselves so they want to be around him. I thought to myself, *I can do this.*

People can only engage in volunteering when they are not at a paying job. Our competition when we recruit is not paid employment; it's whatever the person does in his or her free time. So the choice we're asking people to make is whether to volunteer at church, see a movie, or play golf.

Fun is not the only thing volunteers are looking for, but if they aren't having fun, they won't hang around for very long.

Bottom line—kids' ministry needs to be fun for volunteers too.

I love September at my church. September is when we launch our small groups for the upcoming season. I ask my small-group leaders to make a weekly commitment for nine months, but then I give them the summer off.

At first, I was concerned that my small-group leaders would not come back in the fall if I gave them the summer off, but it had the reverse effect. I retained over 90 percent of my leaders. They looked forward to coming back in the fall because they missed their community.

It was great fun to watch them greeting one another on the first Sunday in September. You literally can feel the love in the room. This makes my job a lot easier because they are pulling on each other. They aren't coming back to see me; they are coming back for each other. Love for one another is the glue that makes it all work.

Chapter 29

Recruiting That Really Works

If you talk to most kidmin pastors, they will tell you that recruiting volunteers is the most stressful part of their job. Part of the reason for the stress is that many kids' pastors spend much of their time on things that don't work.

First of all, let's talk about what doesn't work.

- Bulletin announcements don't work.

- Pulpit announcements don't work.

- Guilt doesn't work.

- Begging doesn't work either.

What does work?

This is what the Holy Spirit said to me early in my ministry:

"Never beg for workers. Let people experience the anointing that is on the kids' ministry, and let Me draw them to you."

There is a calling or an anointing for kids' ministry. The call comes from the Father. You are not the only one in your church that is called. There are others; they just don't know it yet. The key is to leverage opportunities for the entire congregation to experience what you experience every Sunday—the love of the Father for the kids in your class.

One of the challenges in recruiting for kids' ministry is that it is a hidden ministry. People don't know how good it is. Your job is to make the kids' ministry more visible.

Making Kids' Ministry More Visible

The absolute best way to make kids' ministry more visible is to ask your pastor to minister for one service on a Sunday morning.

If he says yes, you can do one of two things:

- A live kids' service in big church
- Preach and cast vision for the kids' ministry

People respond to vision, and people respond to passion.

When I asked my pastor for a Sunday-morning service, he said yes, but then he looked at me and said, "It better be good." The bottom line is if you get a service in the sanctuary, it better be good.

If it's not good, it will have the reverse effect.

- Volunteers will stay away.
- You may not get another chance.
- You will be communicating a negative experience to your pastor.

How do you make it good?

- Be prepared.
- Practice hard.

- Trust the Holy Spirit.
- Work like it all depends on you, and pray like it all depends on God.

If your pastor says no, then ask for five minutes on a Sunday morning or perhaps during a Wednesday-night service. If the five minutes go well, it builds trust. He might give you the whole service next time.

Ask people to get involved.

Another productive way to recruit people is to simply ask them face-to-face to help. It's ironic, but volunteers rarely just volunteer. Most people need to be asked one-on-one.

I go after the new parents that just started attending for three or four weeks. This is how I ask them: "I've noticed that your kids are great kids. They are well-behaved and participate in service. I can tell that you are the kind of parents that I want to teach other people's kids."

Ask people to help with VBS or kids' camp.

Many people do not want to make a long-term commitment, but they will get involved with something, like camp, VBS, or a lock in.

This gives them an opportunity to experience how fun children's ministry is.

This gives you an opportunity to build a relationship during the week. After the event is over, ask them to volunteer in kids' ministry.

I always get new volunteers for kids' ministry from these special events.

Chapter 30

On-the-Job Training

One day I took a look at how we were training our volunteers, and I was not happy with what I observed. It seemed like I was so focused on recruiting new volunteers that I was not doing a good job training the new people we recruited.

So I asked Aaron, a former restaurant manager who was one of my leaders, to help me develop a volunteer-training program. Restaurant managers are constantly training new help, so my thinking was that we could adopt some of their strategies to train new volunteers at church.

Imagine for a minute that you are applying for a job at a restaurant. If you show up during the dinner rush, what is the manager going to do? He's going to ask you to come back at a different time.

The problem with church is we don't have the luxury to ask volunteers to come back on Monday. You need to learn how to conduct your interviews and hire volunteers during the "dinner rush."

The biggest change we made was to hire a volunteer specialist. This is someone who is at every service, strictly for the purpose of connecting with and signing up new volunteers. He or she doesn't teach kids or do check-in. The job involves only three things: sign up new volunteers, guide them through the interview process, and connect them with a ministry.

This is the system that we came up with:

1. Volunteer Specialist

I hired a part-time person to be the volunteer specialist at the three weekend services. Everyone understands that if someone wants to volunteer to help in kids' ministry, we connect him or her with the volunteer specialist—right then.

2. Initial Contact

The Volunteer Specialist does a five-minute on-the-spot interview with the new recruit. She gives them an application and background-check form. She also collects the best contact e-mail and phone number for that recruit.

3. Pre-Screen Interview

In the next day or two, the Volunteer Specialist contacts the new recruit and schedules a pre-screen interview. We schedule our interviews around church service times when people are already there. You have to be persistent when making contact, as people are really busy these days. They may not call you back the first time, but that doesn't mean they don't want to get involved.

This is what we do in the pre-screen interview:

- Collect the application and background check.
- Take a photo for the their worker badge. (If they forgot their background check, we give them one to fill out on the spot before we take the photo for the badge.)

- Give them a tour of the children's ministry area.

- Show them where the bathrooms are and explain the no-adults-in-kids'-bathrooms policy.

- Introduce them to the leadership team.

- Schedule the next interview with the kids' pastor.

4. Placement Interview

- I always meet face-to-face with new volunteers.

- I ask them to tell me their story. I want to know how they found the Lord and how they started coming to our church.

- I tell them my story and testimony.

- I go over the qualifications for children's ministry volunteers.

- I go over the safe boundaries for children's ministry.

- I give them their children's ministry badge.

- I connect them with the leader in their area, and then he or she will connect them with the teacher who is going to mentor them.

5. Mentoring

Mentoring can take up to eight weeks. The new volunteer is to follow one of our teachers for four weeks, and then the teacher follows the new volunteer for about four weeks.

Not all of my teachers have a heart for mentoring. I am very selective of whom I ask to be a mentor because he or she will be doing the hands-on training.

Chapter 31

Catch Them Doing Something Right

The first month is very important when training volunteers. Don't just give them instruction and correction, but make sure you catch them doing something right and praise them for it.

I vividly remember my infamous first Sunday teaching in children's church. I was nineteen years old, and I was serving at a church that was experiencing tremendous growth. The children's pastor asked me to help in the preschool class which had eighty 3-, 4-, and 5-year olds in one big room.

Jeanne (the lead teacher) took one look at my fearful disposition and put me out of my misery with the statement, "Why don't you just watch today?"

I nodded my head in relief.

After class, Jeanne gave me an assignment, "I want you to watch this filmstrip." (This was in 1978—long before ProPresenter™, MediaShout™, DVD, or even VHS.)

"I like the art on this filmstrip, but I don't like the story. I want you to rewrite the story and tell it next week."

I was pumped! This was my first time to get up in front of the kids. I began my preparations for the big day.

One week later, I found myself stunned, standing at the front of the class, staring back at the faces of seventy-eight distracted kids and two that were slightly interested. I totally lost the class.

Not knowing how to stop and ask the kids to be quiet, I just kept telling my story and turning the knob on the filmstrip projector.

Negative thoughts raced through my mind. "This is not your calling," and "You stink at this." I was only at the starting gate, and I was already set to quit.

After class, Jeanne approached me with genuine excitement and said, "Oh, you did so well!"

"I did?"

"Yes," she said, "you told the story from your heart. We can really use you!"

I understand now that I didn't do a great job telling my story that day. I know a lot more about storytelling today; however, if Jeanne had tried to bring a lot of correction, I might have quit before I got started.

Jeanne saw something of value inside of me and knew that I needed encouragement on that first day.

When you genuinely praise people for doing well, it motivates them to do more, and it creates an emotional bond with you.

Chapter 32

Training Volunteers
in the 21st Century

People are busier than ever. I used to train my volunteers at monthly meetings on Sunday night, but it's hard to get people to show up for extra meetings.

I had to figure out how to train my volunteers in small doses. Now, I do all of my training in three bite-size nuggets.

1. The Ten-Minute Huddle

We have a ten-minute huddle every Sunday, thirty minutes before the service starts. The Head Coach does the training because I want my leaders looking to their head coach.

She will cover the object lesson for that day, remind everyone about any announcements and policies, and pray with all her leaders. Sometimes we will provide donuts and coffee during this time.

2. VIT (Very Important Training) E-mail

This is five minutes of training in an e-mail format that is sent out weekly.

It usually is three paragraphs or less. I have found that if my teaching doesn't fit on the screen, then most people will not scroll down to read it.

If you don't have a lot of time to create your own training e-mails, you can find plenty of examples in my blog posts (www.superchurch.com), and then you can forward those posts to your volunteers.

3. Monthly Meetings

I meet with my small-group leaders for thirty minutes every month.

We do this during large-group time. I pull my small-group leaders out of large group for training in a separate room.

Participation in my training went from less than 50 percent to 98 percent because I did it when they were already at church.

Chapter 33

Pastoring Your Volunteers

I still remember the day I changed my strategy for recruiting and training volunteers. It was a cold winter morning in 1987, and I had just accepted a new position as a children's pastor at a church in Minneapolis, Minnesota.

I was frustrated because yet another volunteer had informed me he was stepping down. And, like most children's pastors, I was one of the last ones to leave the building.

This memorable day, my pity party was approaching epic proportions when I bumped into the head usher, Phil. When I saw Phil, I thought, "I wish I had the people that Phil has on his team." It seemed to me that the best men in the church were already volunteering as ushers.

I heard that still small voice ask, "Why don't you talk to Phil? Maybe he knows something that you don't know."

I explained my problem to Phil, and then I asked, "What do you do if everybody wants to quit, and it starts a domino effect?"

Phil looked at me with his patented, incontestable gaze and stated, "We don't let our people quit."

"You mean they are in for life?" I asked.

I think Phil was just trying to get my attention. He went on to explain what he meant, "I find when people get involved in serving at church, they stay in church. The reverse is also true. If people don't get involved in ministry, they end up leaving the church. I don't like losing good people, but more importantly, I want them to stay connected to the church. If somebody wants to quit, I always ask: 'What ministry are you going to serve in next?' If they don't know, I stay connected to them until they either come back to the usher ministry or hook up with another ministry."

A light turned on.

> To ask someone to serve in church is in his or her best interest.

Phil wasn't just trying to get something out of people. **He really cared about the spiritual wellbeing of his team**. Phil was doing something that I didn't know how to do. He was pastoring his volunteers.

Shepherd the flock of God among you, exercising oversight not under compulsion, but voluntarily, according to the will of God; and not for sordid gain, but with eagerness; nor yet as lording it over those allotted to your charge, but proving to be examples to the flock.

1 Peter 5:2,3 NASB

Peter offers us three steps needed for pastoring volunteers:

1. Be an example to your volunteers.

A good leader never expects from his followers what he doesn't first expect from himself. I find it surprising how many kidmin pastors never participate in the main service or sit under their pastors' ministry.

Your volunteers are watching your example.

When you are traveling with your children, what do the flight attendants tell you to do if the oxygen masks appear above you? Do you put the mask on your child first? No, you put on your mask first, and then you help your child. If you don't take care of yourself first, you won't have any life left to minister to your child.

The same is true in ministry.

> *Ministry is so busy that I have to fight for my time to attend church, read the Word, and spend quality time in prayer; but if I don't do it, I won't have anything to give to my leaders.*

2. Get a vision for each volunteer.

Think about some of your key volunteers. Where do you see them a year from now? Do you see them always doing the same thing, or can they grow into new positions? Do you see them overcoming their weaknesses?

As I am writing this, I am thinking about a young man named Bill who started volunteering when he was twelve years old. I saw that Bill was creative and had a gift for puppetry. I asked him to join our outreach team. He traveled with us to do kids' crusades at other churches. Bill loved it and was a real asset to the team.

Bill also had some negative qualities. Sometimes he was cocky, which came off as disrespectful, when he would talk to adults; but I never gave up on Bill. Some of the church leaders would say things like, "Why do you take Bill with you on the road? I couldn't stand being with him for five whole days." When I resigned four years later, Bill was sixteen years old, and people were saying, "That Bill sure has a lot to offer."

A good leader is someone who knows how to see the gifts in others when there is little to be seen on the surface. Ask God to show you how to develop individual gifts in others and, in doing so, you will get a vision for each volunteer.

3. Feed your volunteers.

I'm not talking about coffee and donuts. I'm talking about ministering to your volunteers.

Jesus told us to go into all of the world and make disciples of all nations (see Matt. 28:19). The word *disciple* means a taught or trained one.

We can't only train volunteers. We have to feed them the good Word of God.

If kidmin pastors would pour themselves into their volunteers with the same passion they pour themselves into their kids, they wouldn't have any recruiting problems.

The spiritual growth of your kids is limited to the spiritual growth of those volunteers that are ministering to them.

Chapter 34

Family Ministry

We hear a lot of talk today about family ministry, but what exactly is family ministry?

My thoughts about family ministry have changed over thirty-five years of ministry. I have a different view of things than when I started.

This is my definition of family ministry: family ministry is comprised of the church and the home working together to lead our children to Christ and help them grow them into strong Christians.

It's true.

The church and the home are a powerful team.

There are no guarantees in life, but when the church and the home are working together, we will have more success in making disciples of our kids.

A couple of questions you need to ask yourself:

1. What is your pastor's vision for family ministry?

Family ministry begins with the senior pastor's vision. You might be really excited about family ministry and partnering with parents, but if your pastor is not, you might end up hitting your head against the wall.

2. What is the size of your church?

Some of the strategies for family ministry are created for mega churches. The smaller the church, the less need for what we have come to call "family ministry."

Strategies of Family Ministry

The Family Pastor

Many churches are hiring family pastors to oversee all of family ministry from birth to eighteen. The goal here is to get all of kids' ministry and youth ministry on the same page. I think this is a good idea if the church has the resources to hire a family pastor, but the reality is that this is one of those strategies that really only works for mega churches.

Small- to mid-size churches don't have the financial resources to hire a family pastor in addition to a kids' pastor and a youth pastor. I have seen some mid-size churches promote their youth pastor to family pastor, let their kids' pastor go, and run their kids program with all volunteers. Common sense tells you that if you fire your kids' pastor, your kids' program is going to suffer.

For churches under 2,000 people, the senior pastor should fulfill the roll of keeping the youth ministry and kids' ministry on the same page.

Synchronized Lessons

This is another great strategy that works some of the time but not all of the time.

The concept here is for everyone in church from preschool to the sanctuary to be taught the same lesson, same memory verse, same Bible story, etc.

This strategy takes a lot of effort and coordination, but it is worth it! However, it begins with the senior pastor. You are going to have to follow his lead on what to teach. The bottom line is that this only works if it's something that your senior pastor wants to do.

My experience is that you can do synchronized series a couple of times a year, but there are subjects that need to be taught to teenagers that should not be taught to grade-school kids and vice versa.

Take-Home Pages

Take-home pages and/or parent curriculum is another great idea, but my experience is that only 10-20 percent of parents actually use it.

The percentages go up dramatically if the senior pastor will mention them from the pulpit and tell the parents to minister to their children. Either way, I think this is worth the effort. Don't get angry with the parents who just throw them away. Be grateful for the parents who do take the time to minister to their kids.

Family Services

One of the best ways to partner with parents is through a family service. When parents and kids have a shared family experience at church, it's a powerful thing.

There are many different ways to do this.

Some churches have a thirty-minute family service following the Sunday morning service, but this only works if the main service is an hour or less.

If parents have already sat in the main service for ninety minutes, they aren't going to want to hang around with their kids for another thirty minutes.

I have found the best way to get good participation in a family service is to do it once or twice a year on Sunday morning in place of the main service. If your pastor gives you permission to do this, make sure it's really good.

Family VBS

We made a difficult decision to shift the focus of our VBS from a kids' event to a family event. We had 1,000 kids coming to our VBS every year, so this was a hard decision to make because I knew I was going to lose some of the kids to reach the parents.

Here is what we did to change VBS to a family event:

- We moved VBS from the morning to the evening.
- We shortened VBS to a one-hour event.
- Parents could not drop off their kids—they had to participate.

The end result was we still had 1,000 in attendance, but 30 percent of them were parents. This was without a doubt the most successful family ministry event of the year for us.

E-mail/Blog

I know this is incredibly simple, but one of the most effective things I do to engage parents is send out a monthly e-mail/blog post introducing our series for the month and letting them know about any special activities. The key is to keep it *short*.

Anything you can do to get communication going is worth doing.

If you can get parents to engage and respond to your e-mails, you are doing a good job.

Chapter 35

The Best Way to Partner with Parents

I know this is incredibly obvious, but it needs to be said. The best way to partner with parents is to get them involved with the kids' ministry program. In other words, use the kidmin program to disciple the parents.

When we launched small groups for kids at our church, it was a major undertaking. We had 600 grade-school kids on the combined roster for our three Sunday morning services. I wanted ten small groups at each service, so I needed 30 small-group leaders and 30 assistant leaders, but I was starting with 0 small-group leaders.

It took about nine months, but eventually we did get our sixty small-group leaders.

One month during our small-group training, I was going around the room and asking the question, "What do you get out of this ministry?"

The response I heard the most was, "This makes me a better parent."

Then it hit me.

> *I didn't just start a small-group ministry for kids;*
> *I started a parent ministry.*

I have sixty parents that I am training to minister to kids.

After teaching other people's kids, my small-group leaders gained confidence that they could teach their own kids, and now they are doing it at home.

My point is you may not need to start a new ministry to partner with parents; simply leverage the kids' ministry for that purpose.

Chapter 36

Parent Weekend

The Holy Spirit told me early on, "Never beg for workers. Allow people to experience the anointing that is on the kids' ministry, and let Me draw them."

One of the most successful strategies I created to connect with parents is Parent Weekend.

> My goal for Parent Weekend is to allow the parent to experience the anointing that is on the kids' ministry.

My original strategy for Parent Weekend was to use it to recruit new volunteers, but even if they do not get involved, it gives me a way to connect with parents. Plus, it helps the parents understand what our goals are. This alone makes it worth the effort.

Here is what Parent Weekend looks like:

1. I spread Parent Weekend out for an entire month.

I like to do Parent Weekends throughout the month of October. I know it does not look good for a lot of parents to be missing from the sanctuary on the same weekend, so I make a schedule that spreads them out:

1st weekend	>	Parents of 1st graders
2nd weekend	>	Parents of 2nd graders
3rd weekend	>	Parents of 3rd graders
4th weekend	>	Parents of 4th and 5th graders

2. I print up a Parent Weekend brochure.

I hand it out two weeks before the first weekend in October. I also send an e-mail to parents of first graders on the Thursday before the first weekend. (I follow this pattern for the entire month.)

3. When parents of first graders arrived, they stay in the class with their son or daughter.

Most parents sit next to their kids. Right before the offering, I invite the first graders to bring their parents up to the front. I tell them, "Introduce your mom and dad to us, and tell us something that you like about them." Then we clap for all the parents, and I thank them for honoring their kids.

4. Then I have all the second graders stand up, and I remind them that next weekend is their weekend.

Repeat after me: "Mom, Dad, next weekend is Parent Weekend for second grade. Will you come to children's church with me?" Kids are the best promoters for Parent Weekend.

5. **Toward the end of the service, I invite the parents into a hospitality room for coffee and juice.**

We hand out volunteer packets to the parents, and I share our vision. Then I open it up for questions.

(It's a good idea to ask one parent that you know to be prepared to ask a question to help get the questions started.)

6. **We then contact the parents within a few days and ask them to get involved.**

If they are already plugged in as volunteers in another ministry, we don't contact them.

I have found that about 30 percent of the parents who are not already involved in ministry will sign up. The younger the kids, the better chance we have of getting them to sign up, so we really focus on parents of first and second graders.

Chapter 37

There Is a Difference Between Parenting and Pastoring

Pastors and parents have the same goal. We both want to see kids grow into strong Christians, but that does not mean we have the same job. Unity is not everybody doing and saying the same thing; it is everybody having the same goal.

Synergy is not sameness; it is honoring one another's differences.

When I first started in ministry, I began to recognize spiritual gifts in kids that their own parents didn't necessarily see.

I asked Pastor Willie George about it one day, and he responded, "This happens because most parents see their kids after the flesh."

Think about it. When the prophet Samuel showed up at Jesse's home to anoint a new king for Israel, Jesse brought out seven sons, and the Lord rejected them all.

The Lord said to Samuel, "God sees not as man sees, for man looks on the outward appearance but the Lord looks on the heart" (1 Sam. 16:7 NASB).

Jesse didn't see the gift in his own son David because he was looking on David's outward appearance.

There may be young Davids in your class who have not yet been discovered— this is part of your calling!

Remember, there is a difference between parenting and pastoring.

Here's something else I've observed to be true. As a pastor, I may be in a better position to present the Gospel to the kids in my class. Please don't misunderstand me. I'm not saying that parents shouldn't present the Gospel to their own children.

I'm simply suggesting the church may be more effective in presenting the Gospel to children than their parents, and here's why:

Parents spend a big portion of their time trying to get kids to obey, to follow the rules, to clean their rooms, and do their homework.

One key to getting kids to obey you is to be consistent with your discipline. If your son or daughter breaks the rules, there is a price to pay—perhaps a spanking or a loss of privilege. **In other words, kids learn to obey out of fear of the penalty.**

The Gospel is an entirely different message. The Gospel says that Jesus paid the price for our disobedience. In other words, God spanked Jesus instead of spanking me. Yes, it makes God angry when I sin, but He poured out His anger on Jesus when He was on the cross.

One problem is that we mix the scriptures on evangelism and parenting, and we tend to think they are the same when it comes to children.

You can make your child clean his room or do her homework, but you cannot make them have a relationship with Christ. That is something they have to choose to do because they love Jesus.

As a pastor, my job is not to try to get the kids to obey the rules. If I focus too much on obeying the rules, it can become a form of legalism. My job is to lead kids to Christ and allow their obedience to flow from their love for Christ.

My point is this: do not confuse parenting classes with the Gospel.

The church should offer parenting classes, and the church should preach the Gospel; but they are not the same thing.

Chapter 38

It Is All About Who You Know

"It's all about who you know": I first heard this statement from a pastor's wife.

She was commenting on how her denomination was too political. The inference was that people were promoted to positions of leadership, not based on their character or abilities, but simply on whom their friends were.

Admittedly, this does happen; however, if you receive a promotion simply based on friendship and don't have the necessary abilities, you won't have that job for very long.

On the other hand, if you don't have any relationships, you may never get a shot at a job that you really want. All things being equal, people will do business with someone they know and like.

The truth is that whom you know is a key part of what makes life work. It's also a key part of what makes church work.

My best friends are people who serve at my church or serve at another church. They are people that I genuinely care about. I want to see them succeed, and they want to see me succeed.

Networking is like breathing. It's not the only thing that matters, but if you don't do it, you won't last very long.

Networking means different things to different people.

According to Webster, *networking* is defined as "the developing of contacts with others in an informal network, as to further a career."

I asked my daughter, Missy, how she would define *networking*, and she said, "It's like making friends." (I like both definitions.)

Networking is the intersection between work and friendship. For the purpose of this book, I am defining networking as building friendships with like-minded people where you can help fulfill each others' goals.

You may be asking, "How do I get started with networking?"

1. Start with leaders in your own church.

Make a list of the most influential leaders in your church, and have coffee with them. The networking you do within your own church is the most important.

2. Participate in events at your church that are not sponsored by the children's ministry.

Attend the ladies' meetings and the men's retreats. If the greeters don't recognize you, don't blame them. Maybe you need to get out more. (Just a thought.)

3. Connect with other children's pastors in your state.

I know you are busy, but pick up the phone and make the call. You will be glad you did. Every lunch is an opportunity to meet another like-minded leader.

4. Participate in networking sites.

Take advantage of social-media websites. Be careful not to get addicted, but use it as a great way to connect with like-minded people.

5. Go to conferences.

One of the best places to meet influential people is at conferences. I make a point to attend at least one conference per year. Many times it has not been in my church's budget, so I paid for it myself.

Why would I pay for a conference out of my own pocket? I love making new friends that have a heart for ministry! I have developed lifelong relationships with friends that I met at conferences.

Chapter 39

The Ten Commandments of Networking

1. Think win/win.

Any relationship that God is a part of is mutually benefiting.

2. Lead by asking questions.

Come prepared with written questions.

3. Think about the other guy first.

What can you do to help him or her?

4. Listen more; talk less.

Be quick to hear and slow to speak.

5. Be a giver.

Find something of value that you can give away.

6. Avoid talking about politics and theological differences.

You can learn from anybody, regardless of his or her theology.

7. **Turn lunchtime into the most productive hour of the day.**

Take somebody to lunch.

8. **Don't be afraid to ask for help.**

The worst thing they can say is no.

9. **Give people space.**

Don't be too clingy. If you are at a conference, meet somebody new and then meet somebody else.

10. **Get outside of your circle.**

The body of Christ is a bunch of little circles. If you get to know someone in a new circle, he or she can introduce you to many new friends.

Chapter 40

How to Get Along with Your Youth Pastor

I was sitting at a children's minister conference one year listening to a group of kids' pastors trashing the youth pastors in their respective churches. I really wanted to correct them or slap them, but I bit my tongue. I learned long ago to not give advice if I think people will not listen.

Other than the senior pastor, the youth pastor is your most important relationship in the church. But let's be honest. Youth pastors can be challenging to get along with. They seem to be cut from a different mold than the other leaders. The bottom line is if I do not have a good relationship with the youth pastor, it is not good for the kids in my church.

Think about it. Every child you teach is heading to the youth ministry. They are all becoming teenagers, and there is nothing you can do to stop it.

We need to start thinking long term. One of my goals is that the children I am ministering to will make the jump to the youth ministry, and then they will stay in our church when they graduate from high school.

As kids' pastors, we need to do everything possible to create a smooth transition to the youth ministry. If we see children sitting in the sanctuary because they don't like the youth ministry, it's their first step away from church.

When was the last time you talked to the youth pastor? If it's been a while, take him or her out to lunch and start building a strong relationship.

How to Cultivate a Healthy Relationship with Your Youth Pastor

1. Seek to understand and then be understood. The key to influencing other leaders is to allow yourself to be influenced by them.

2. Never criticize the youth pastor. You will have parents come to you and tell you what they don't like about the youth ministry. Don't listen to them. Do not agree with them. If they have a problem with the youth ministry, they need to talk to the youth pastor.

3. Plan some activities just for fifth graders, and invite the youth pastor to come along.

4. Once or twice a year invite the youth band and youth pastor to minister in children's church.

5. Encourage your fifth-grade small-group leaders to make the jump to youth ministry with the kids in their small groups.

Chapter 41

The Lone-Ranger Syndrome

Do you ever feel like the whole church is backslidden because somebody moved your DVD player?

I know I've had that thought before.

One of the greatest enemies of kids' pastors is the Lone-Ranger Syndrome.

Do you have thoughts like this: "The other leaders in our church do not have a vision for the children."

The other day, the Holy Spirit asked me, "Do you support their vision?"

With my *words*, I supported the other pastors in my church, but my *actions* told another story.

When I thought about it, the only ministry I was involved in was children's ministry. Like everybody else, I thought I had lots of good reasons to not help other people with their visions.

One day I was complaining to the leader of our men's ministry because very few of the men in his group were serving in children's ministry. He replied, "Mark, have you ever attended the men's retreat or participated in men's ministry?"

At that point I had to eat humble pie.

I did something that year that I had never done before. I took a weekend off and attended the men's retreat. It's hard to believe, but in thirty years of serving in churches, I had never attended a men's retreat.

I had a great time, renewed some old friendships, and I communicated to the other pastors in my church that I support their vision.

The best way to gain influence with other leaders is to allow yourself to be influenced by them.

If you have been running with your vision and it seems like you have hit an invisible wall, maybe it's time to support someone else's vision.

Great leaders know how to work with other leaders.

If you don't know how to work with other leaders, it becomes a lid on your leadership in the church. You won't have any influence outside of the kids' ministry.

Chapter 42

Leading Up

As a kids' pastor, it's critical that you know how to lead up. When I talk about leading up, I am talking about having influence with people that outrank you—your pastor, supervisor, or the church board.

Is it possible to lead when you are not the top dog?

The answer is a resounding yes!

Leadership doesn't always start at the top, but it always manages to affect the people at the top.

The story of David and Goliath is a great example of leading up. David wasn't even enlisted in the army and yet he managed to have influence over the commander in chief:

As soon as the Israelite army saw him, they began to run away in fright.

"Have you seen the giant?" the men asked. "He comes out each day to defy Israel. The king has offered a huge reward to anyone who kills him. He will give that man one of his daughters for a wife, and the man's entire family will be exempted from paying taxes!"

David asked the soldiers standing nearby, "What will a man get for killing this Philistine and ending his defiance of Israel? Who is this pagan Philistine anyway, that he is allowed to defy the armies of the living God?"

And these men gave David the same reply. They said, "Yes, that is the reward for killing him."

But when David's oldest brother, Eliab, heard David talking to the men, he was angry. "What are you doing around here anyway?" he demanded. "What about those few sheep you're supposed to be taking care of? I know about your pride and deceit. You just want to see the battle!"

"What have I done now?" David replied. "I was only asking a question!"

He walked over to some others and asked them the same thing and received the same answer. Then David's question was reported to King Saul, and the king sent for him.

"Don't worry about this Philistine," David told Saul. "I'll go fight him!"

"Don't be ridiculous!" Saul replied. "There's no way you can fight this Philistine and possibly win! You're only a boy, and he's been a man of war since his youth."

But David persisted. "I have been taking care of my father's sheep and goats," he said. "When a lion or a bear comes to steal a lamb from the flock, I go after it with a club and rescue the lamb from its mouth. If the animal turns on me, I catch it by the jaw and club it to death. I have done this to both lions and bears, and I'll do it to this pagan Philistine, too, for he has defied the armies of the living God! The Lord who rescued me from the claws of the lion and the bear will rescue me from this Philistine!"

Saul finally consented. "All right, go ahead," he said. "And may the Lord be with you!"

Then Saul gave David his own armor—a bronze helmet and a coat of mail.

David put it on, strapped the sword over it, and took a step or two to see what it was like, for he had never worn such things before.

"I can't go in these," he protested to Saul. "I'm not used to them." So David took them off again. He picked up five smooth stones from a stream and put them into his shepherd's bag. Then, armed only with his shepherd's staff and sling, he started across the valley to fight the Philistine.

Goliath walked out toward David with his shield bearer ahead of him, sneering in contempt at this ruddy-faced boy. "Am I a dog," he roared at David, "that you come at me with a stick?" And he cursed David by the names of his gods. "Come over here, and I'll give your flesh to the birds and wild animals!" Goliath yelled.

David replied to the Philistine, "You come to me with sword, spear, and javelin, but I come to you in the name of the Lord of Heaven's Armies—the God of the armies of Israel, whom you have defied. Today the Lord will conquer you, and I will kill you and cut off your head. And then I will give the dead bodies of your men to the birds and wild animals, and the whole world will know that there is a God in Israel! And everyone assembled here will know that the Lord rescues his people, but not with sword and spear. This is the Lord's battle, and he will give you to us!"

As Goliath moved closer to attack, David quickly ran out to meet him.

Reaching into his shepherd's bag and taking out a stone, he hurled it with his sling and hit the Philistine in the forehead. The stone sank in, and Goliath stumbled and fell face down on the ground.

So David triumphed over the Philistine with only a sling and a stone, for he had no sword.

1 Samuel 17:24-50

There are ten principles we can learn from David about leading up:

1. Seek to understand and then be understood.

David understood Saul's problem: "Who is this uncircumcised Philistine that he should defy the armies of the living God?" (1 Sam. 17:26 KJV).

Understanding is more than intellectual knowledge. Understanding means that you feel the same emotions that your leader feels. Not only was this a potential military defeat, this was an embarrassment to the king. David felt what Saul felt.

Many people that serve in youth and/or children's ministry do not feel that their pastors understand them. The key to getting someone to understand you is for you to understand him or her first.

The key to influencing someone that outranks you is for you to allow yourself to be influenced by him or her.

It speaks volumes to a parent when a child says, "Mom, I like this church."

At my first church, we had ages 3 to 12 in one room as we were just starting out. One Sunday, I did the lesson on the sword of the Spirit where I chop apples with a giant machete. On this particular Sunday, I had a new three-year-old girl named Brooke. I was a little concerned what Brooke thought about the machete, but she seemed to do okay.

I was relieved to see the family return to church the following week. Her dad mentioned to me that when they were getting ready for church that morning, Brooke spoke up, "Mom, Dad, I want to go to the apple-slicing church."

When you hear a testimony like this, make sure your pastor and church board hear about it.

An effective kids' ministry will bring your visitors back, and this is something that will motivate your pastor.

2. Deal with criticism.

As soon as David started to lead, his older brother took a shot at him.

When you gain influence with your leader, other people may take shots at you. If you are getting shot at, it just means that you are leading. Don't take it personally, and don't shoot back. All leaders get shot at. It just comes with the territory. You need to develop thick skin and a soft heart.

How did David respond to his brother?

- He ignored him and kept his focus on the enemy.

- David knew who the enemy was, and it wasn't his brother.

- David didn't get lured into someone else's battle.

3. Keep your motives pure.

David's motives were pure: "Is there not a cause?" (1 Sam. 17:29 KJV). He was not self-promoting.

If there is any hint of self-promotion, you lose credibility. It's a good thing to ask for resources if your motives are pure. For the church, our cause is the mission of Christ—to seek and save the lost.

4. Lead by asking questions.

It's a tricky thing to lead up. You need to be humble and confident at the same time. What did David do? He asked questions that he already knew the answer to: "He walked over to some others and asked them the same thing and received the same answer" (1 Sam. 17:30).

Be a problem solver, but don't come to your leader with one solution.

Never present your leader with an ultimatum. I find that pastors like multiple-choice tests. This lets them make the choice.

Most pastors are type-A personalities, and they like to be in control. By presenting a problem with several solutions, it shows your pastor you are proactive and diligent.

5. Know when the door is open.

Respect your leader's time. Pastors are busy people. Wait until he is asking questions: "David's questions was reported to King Saul, and the king sent for him" (1 Sam. 17:31).

You know that the door is open when your leader is asking questions.

If your leader's first response is no, don't force the issue. Let it go. Your leader may change his or her mind later.

6. Don't try to lead up unless you are willing to fight the giant.

It's easy to identify problems. It's another thing to solve them. One thing I appreciate about my pastor is that he asks for our suggestions in staff meeting. Early on, I would freely give my input and identify problems.

Pastor would usually respond with, "Mark, why don't you take care of that?"

I learned to not bring up problems if I were not willing to go to battle.

7. Be confident.

Don't be cocky, but you do need to be confident. Know what your strengths are. Your strengths are things you have done before with success.

David did not use Saul's armor because it affected his confidence. David's confidence was in God, but it was also in his ability to use a slingshot.

8. Do it afraid.

David had to be dealing with some level of fear when Goliath roared at him: "Come here, and I'll give your flesh to the birds and the wild animals" (1 Sam. 17:44 NIV).

Confidence is not the absence of fear.

I love this quote from Steven Pressfield: "The more scared we are of a work or a calling, the more sure we can be that we have to do it."

9. Think positive thoughts, and say positive words.

We all deal with negative thoughts, but negative thoughts do not come from the Lord. I find that even when the Lord is correcting me, He does it in an encouraging way. So when I think negative thoughts, I realize that these are not His thoughts.

What did David do when he was dealing with fearful thoughts? He spoke positive words, and he went for a run. I do the same thing: I go for a run, and I say positive words. Many times I speak scriptures while I am running.

Seriously though, many psychiatrists say that exercise works better than medication if you are dealing with depression.

Bottom line: if you are going into battle, stay positive.

10. Get results.

David got results. If Goliath had won, this story would not be in the Bible.

You need to get results too. Pastors like results.

Bear fruit in areas that motivate your pastor. Don't always come to your pastor with problems. (If you see your pastor duck into his office when he sees you coming, you have a problem.)

When we did our first family service on a Sunday morning, I did a lot of advertising. I gave out a cool prize for the child who brought the most friends. We had a full house, but more importantly, we had over a hundred first-time visitors. I asked all of the first-time visitors to come up to the front so I could give them a visitor packet. They all had to walk by my pastor. I knew this would be a blessing to him.

When you get a good report from a parent, make sure to e-mail it to your pastor. You know the complaints are coming his way, so make sure he gets the good news too.

Chapter 43

Let's Talk About Money

A lot of kids' pastors are naïve when it comes to money. They think that ministry is all spiritual. Trust me on this: your pastor is thinking about money every day. Yes, your pastor is the primary preacher in your church, but in most instances, he is also the primary fundraiser. He is the one carrying the burden for the finances. If it's not your pastor, it's your church board, but someone is carrying the financial responsibility. You want to have influence with those people.

My point is this: you need to know how to talk to your leader about money in a way that communicates you get it. Most pastors are not motivated about the kids' ministry. Your pastor may not even be thinking about the kids.

So quit begging for money. Instead ask yourself what motivates your pastor.

For example, many pastors are motivated by growth, and the experts tell us that kids' ministry is number three on the list of things that people think about when choosing a church.

Now you have something to work with.

Don't view kids' ministry as an *expense*. Kids' ministry is an *investment*.

If a visitor comes with a six-month-old child, and the church nursery is full, that visitor is not coming back. It doesn't matter how big the sanctuary is. The size of the church is limited by the size of the nursery.

If your classrooms fill up because they aren't big enough, don't get upset. Leverage it for growth.

At my most recent church, I had been talking to my pastor and church board for over a year because we were totally full in kids' church. My words didn't seem to get any traction, but I kept at it.

Then one Sunday in January, it happened. We had to turn away some parents at the 11:00 a.m. service because there was no room. We were way past fire code.

Some board members were coming to me saying, "You can't turn kids away."

"What do you suggest I do?" was my response.

For three weeks in a row, we had to turn kids away.

After that, the new kids' building became part of the stewardship campaign, and I didn't need to say a word.

Chapter 44

7 Things Pastors Hate

Not only do you need to know what motivates your pastor or supervisor, you need to know what bugs them.

Do you know what your pastor's pet peeves are?

If you don't, you are going to hit some bumps in your ministry.

Every leader is different. Personalities vary. However, I have found seven things that all pastors dislike. (Please don't ask how I found out this vital information.)

Here is my list (in no particular order):

1. **Passing the Buck**

   If you make a mistake, own up to it. Don't defend yourself, and don't play the blame game. Practice saying these words, "I messed up, and I will fix the problem."

2. **Conflict with Other Staff**

   If you are on staff at a church, you will have conflict with other leaders. Conflict is part of life.

   Be big enough to resolve your own conflict.

Your pastor has enough problems without you bringing more problems his way. Have a plan for conflict resolution. If what you are doing isn't working, then ask someone for help.

3. Talking About Your Former Church

Pastors don't like it when a new staff person continually brings up, "This is how they did it at my last church."

It may be appropriate if your pastor is asking for input, but it's probably best to say it like this: "I've seen it done this way before."

4. Inflexibility

In ministry, we need to be flexible.

It's best not to say to your pastor, "We *have* to do it this way."

If you see a problem, come to your pastor with several solutions. Pastors like multiple-choice tests.

5. Correction

Your pastor has shortcomings and weaknesses. It doesn't take too long to figure out what they are, but it's not your job to change him. He has people in his life to speak to him.

Understand that you wear different hats with your pastor. Sometimes he is speaking to you as your pastor—he may be asking for input, but sometimes he is speaking to you as your boss.

As your employer, your pastor's job is to correct you, but it's not your job to correct him or her.

I had an employee once who used to deflect my correction back to me instead of receiving it. Whenever he messed up, somehow it was always my bad. Big mistake. If you do get corrected, your pastor is looking for a response like this: "I hear what you are saying, and I will change."

At one of our conferences, a fellow kids' pastor made this statement to me.

"I am really frustrated with my pastor."

"How come?" I asked.

"He is really disorganized, and I am not."

"Maybe that is why you are there—to help him."

"Oh, I get it now," he said.

For some crazy reason, we expect pastors to be strong in every area, but they are not. That's why they hire staff.

6. Saying Stupid Things from the Pulpit

Most pastors do a good job at creating their own controversy. They don't need you creating more.

When you have an opportunity to speak in front of the whole church, don't blow it. Think about what you are going to say. You want to get more opportunities in the pulpit.

7. Disloyalty

Pastors don't like it when you talk to people in the congregation about what's wrong with your church.

If you need to talk to somebody (and we all do at times), call a friend in another state.

Most of us have done these things at some point in our ministries. The important thing is that we learn from our mistakes and keep running our race. The cause of Christ is too important.

Chapter 45

The Call of the Father

Your call is a precious thing to the Father.

If you've just finished reading this book, then you know there is a lot of work involved in leading a kids' program in a local church; but at the end of the day, it is all about the kids and connecting them with their Heavenly Father.

I was a kids' pastor for fifteen years before I really understood the heart of the Father for His kids. Intellectually, I understood that Father God loves the kids that I taught, but I didn't really *get* it.

I remember the day that everything changed for me.

I was attending a special service at another church in town. It was toward the end of the service, and the worship team began singing a song entitled "So Come" by Kevin Prosch.

(Sometimes God will speak to me through pictures. For example, during prayer I will see faces of people I need to pray for. I have learned to follow these prayer cues.)

I had my eyes closed as I sang the words about how God is a father to a lonely child. While I was singing, I saw a picture of a young boy who looked to be eight-years old. The boy was sitting by himself inside a dark and gloomy house, looking out a picture window at kids playing outside. He had this really sad look on his face. It was clear that this boy had been left alone.

My first thought was one of human sympathy. Then suddenly from above and behind the boy, I saw a bright light from heaven shine on him. When the light hit him, I felt what God felt.

It's impossible to describe in words the emotions I felt, but for one brief moment, I felt God's heart for the fatherless.

I began to pray and weep for the fatherless children in our nation. The burden of prayer that I had for the fatherless was so strong I literally couldn't stop praying.

Debbie looked at me and asked, "What's wrong?"

I could not talk. I couldn't convey to her what I had seen. I just kept praying and weeping for about twenty minutes.

As a kids' pastor, I have always seen myself as an extension of the lead pastor (which is true); however, most importantly a kids' pastor is an extension of the Father's heart to the kids, especially those who do not have a father at home.

If God is a father to the fatherless, how will they know unless we demonstrate His love in a practical way?

What do your kids need?

They need you to be there for them—just like you have been doing week after week.

The kids you teach know that when they go to church, you will be there for them, to hug them, love on them, and pray for them. They can count on you, and that teaches them that they can count on Father God.

If you've just finished reading this book, then you know there is a lot of work involved in leading a kids program in a local church, but at the end of the day, it is all about the kids and connecting them with their Heavenly Father.

The bottom line is this: the reason that all of this effort is worth it is because your Heavenly Father likes kids.

Keep doing what you are doing.
Answer the call, run your race, and finish your course.
You are a conduit of the Father's love.

About the Author

Pastor, Filmmaker and Coach, Mark Harper has 35 years of experience in the local church. He is the creator of the Super Church 2.0 Curriculum, which is used in over 5,000 churches worldwide. The focus of Mark's ministry is helping leaders build strong churches and helping parents build strong families. Not only has Mark served in the local church as pastor, associate pastor, and family ministry pastor but he is also a certified coach with the John Maxwell Team.